The Noble
HORSE

The Noble
HORSE

Contributing Editor
FERN COLLINS

CHARTWELL
BOOKS

Inspiring | Educating | Creating | Entertaining

Brimming with creative inspiration, how-to projects, and useful information to enrich your everyday life, Quarto Knows is a favorite destination for those pursuing their interests and passions. Visit our site and dig deeper with our books into your area of interest: Quarto Creates, Quarto Cooks, Quarto Homes, Quarto Lives, Quarto Drives, Quarto Explores, Quarto Gifts, or Quarto Kids.

This edition published in 2016 by
CHARTWELL BOOKS
an imprint of The Quarto Group
142 West 36th Street, 4th Floor
New York, NY 10018, USA

Copyright © 2016 Regency House Publishing Limited
The Manor House
High Street, Buntingford
Hertfordshire, SG9 9AB
United Kingdom

10 9 8 7 6 5 4 3

ISBN-13: 978-0-7858-3478-6

Printed in China

MIX
Paper from
responsible sources
FSC® C008047
www.fsc.org

For all editorial enquiries, please contact:
www.regencyhousepublishing.com

Images used under license from ©Shutterstock.com

In most English speaking countries, the height of a horse is measured in hands. A hand is a unit of measurement of length standardized to 4 inches (101.6 mm). Hands are usually abbreviated to "hh" as they have been in this book.

Having This Day My Horse

Sir Philip Sidney

Having this day my horse, my hand, my lance
Guided so well that I obtain'd the prize,
Both by the judgment of the English eyes
And of some sent from that sweet enemy France;
Horsemen my skill in horsemanship advance,
Town folks my strength; a daintier judge applies
His praise to sleight which from good use doth rise;
Some lucky wits impute it but to chance;
Others, because of both sides I do take
My blood from them who did excel in this,
Think Nature me a man of arms did make.
How far they shot awry! The true cause is,
Stella look'd on, and from her heav'nly face
Sent forth the beams which made so fair my race.

CONTENTS

INTRODUCTION

It has taken nearly 60 million years for the horse to evolve from Eohippus, the Dawn Horse, to the modern horse we know and love today. Horse-lovers do not need to be reminded of the debt they owe *Equus caballus*, but to others, this may not be so immediately apparent. While the horse has been eulogized and has on occasion even assumed mythical proportions, it is at heart a practical creature. While it has achieved harmony with mankind, it has never forgotten its place within the natural world.

In a sense, the horse can be seen as man's traveling companion through life, and this is a task he has accepted with generosity and grace over many thousands of years.

This American Mustang is a feral horse descended from domesticated breeds.

OPPOSITE: The Przewalski's Horse has never been domesticated and remains the only truly wild horse in the world today.

The horse, more than any other animal, has had the strongest connections with human history, and his influence on our culture has been profound. Before the dawning of the mechanical and industrial age, he was indispensable to man: while he was sharing our lives on a domestic level, he was also a beast of burden and a method of transport. From carrying conquering armies into battle, he has made the seamless transition to his latest incarnation as an athlete, and now excels in sport and competition.

Wild horses were first domesticated in Eastern Europe and the Near East about 5,000 years ago, and by 1000 BC, could be found all over Europe, Asia, and North Africa, all having evolved from three primeval types.

The Arabian originates from ancient bloodlines.

OPPOSITE: The Konik, a primitive breed from Poland, is the closest relative of the extinct Tarpan.

These were *Equus caballus sylvaticus*, the Forest Horse, *Equus caballus przewalskii* (the Asiatic Horse), and *Equus caballus gomellini*, the Tarpan, which exists as a protected species to this day.

Indigenous prehistoric horses were once also present in the Americas, but one day they inexplicably disappeared and why this happened has never been discovered. It was the Spanish conquistadors who reintroduced their Iberian horses to the Americas and these continued to evolve in a different way from horses elsewhere. The early pioneers needed horses of great hardiness and stamina and their own horses evolved accordingly; bloodlines from other countries were later imported to improve and refine.

Many of the heavier breeds are descended from horses originally used in battle, carrying knights in heavy armor. These horses were usually bred and raised for the needs of war. They were powerful, agile, and brave.

Today, modern breeding methods have produced the ultimate sporthorse. It is usually bred from coldblooded horses, such as Shires, crossed with hotbloods such as the Thoroughbred. These warmbloods are bred exclusively for sporting purposes, such as show jumping, eventing, and

The Thoroughbred is a hotblood known for its agility, speed, and stamina.

OPPOSITE: Warmbloods are a group of middle-weight breeds developed by crossing hotbloods and coldbloods.

dressage. They are not for work on the farm, but have been produced exclusively for people to enjoy and engage in competition. Well-known sporthorses include the Hanoverian, Trakhener, American Warmblood, and Holstein.

The Noble Horse does not include every breed in existence today, but those that are featured all celebrate the strength and beauty of the horse through all its many guises.

WILD & FERAL HORSES

Mankind's encounters with horses, throughout much of history, have been with the domesticated kind, for the horse has lived side by side with us for thousands of years. Once used as warhorses, as beasts of burden, and for transporting human beings, the horse's modern-day purpose seems to be solely for our pleasure, all of which are a far cry from its true evolution as a wild, free-roaming herd animal.

Naturally gregarious and highly social, horses are at their happiest with others of their kind, surrounded by plenty of open space, so it is hardly surprising that once freedom is allowed they should revert to natural behavior. In the wild, horses form themselves into a herd, with a dominant stallion as their leader, which protects its group of mares and youngsters. The herd forms a close unit, its members playing, grooming, feeding, and resting together, all the while keeping a watchful eye for signs of danger. During the mating season, the stallion will fight for herd dominance,

securing for itself plenty of breeding females in the process.

Horses have evolved to be perfectly adapted to living in the open. They are powerful sprinters capable of achieving significant speeds when fleeing from danger. They have large eyes, set on the sides of their heads, which provide almost all-round vision.

OPPOSITE: The wild Przewalski's Horse.

Feral horses are found all over the world and examples include the Camargue, the Brumby, and the Mustang.

They also have extremely good hearing, and their mobile, pointed ears allow them to catch sounds from all angles.

The instinct to herd provides the group with relative safety compared with that of a lone animal; a galloping group tends to confuse would-be predators, while any animal that is brought down would more likely be one that is weak or sick.

The term "wild horse" is also used colloquially to refer to free-roaming herds of feral horses such as the Mustang in the United States, the Brumby in Australia, and many others. These feral horses are untamed members of the domestic horse subspecies (*Equus ferus caballus*) and should not be confused with the two truly "wild" horse subspecies, the Tarpan or Eurasian Wild Horse (*Equus ferus ferus*), once native to Europe and western Asia, and Przewalski's Horse (*Equus ferus przewalskii*).

OPPOSITE: Camargue horses roam wild in the Rhône delta of south-western France.

BRUMBY

The Brumby is a free-roaming feral horse, descended from horses brought to Australia by early European settlers who arrived in the early 19th century.

During the First World War, many of the horses escaped or were turned loose to run wild: these were the forefathers of the modern-day Brumby, a name said to have been derived from the aboriginal word for "wild" (*baroomby*).

Because of the variety of animals that reverted to a wild state, there is no specific breed type; consequently Brumbies come in all shapes, sizes, and colors.

The horses are now almost totally feral, making them difficult to catch and almost impossible to train. They are prolific breeders and for this reason, in the past, have come to be regarded as pests. This has led to such extensive culling that they are now quite rare. They come in all colors and patterns. Height is up to 15 hh.

OPPOSITE: Although found in many areas around the country, the best-known Brumbies are found in the Australian Alps region in south-eastern Australia.

CAMARGUE

The marshes and wetlands of the Rhône delta, located south of Arles in France, are home to a race of semi-wild horses that spend their time grazing the sparse vegetation. This is a very ancient breed that bears a striking resemblance to the primitive horses painted on cave-walls at Lascaux in prehistoric times. The Camargue's qualities were appreciated by Roman invaders on their way to the Iberian Peninsula, with the result that connections were inevitably made with Spanish breeds.

The breed was further enhanced in the 19th century by infusions of Postier Breton, Arab, Thoroughbred, and Anglo-Arab bloodlines, though they seem to have had little bearing on the horses' overall appearance.

There is a round-up in the Camargue every year, when suitable horses are selected for riding purposes and substandard animals are culled: this may seem ruthless but there is no doubt that it has led to improvements in the breed.

Camargue horses are traditionally ridden by the *gardiens* (Camargue cowboys), who use them for herding the famous black bulls of the region and for festivals in which their dazzling feats of horsemanship are

displayed. The horses are also used for trekking the region, now a popular tourist attraction.

The head of the Camargue (Camarguais) is rather square, with a broad forehead, short, broad ears, and expressive eyes. The neck is short and well-developed, the shoulder upright, and the back is short with a low-set tail. The legs are strong and the hooves well-shaped and tough. The mane and tail are particularly abundant.

Camargues make obedient riding horses; they are extremely agile and have the ability to turn sharply at full gallop. As trekking ponies they are sure-footed and have plenty of stamina. They never quite lose their independent spirit, however, and something of their wild inheritance is always retained. They are invariably white (gray), though other colors sometimes appear. Foals are born dark but their coats grow lighter as they mature. Height is from 13.1–14.2 hh.

OPPOSITE: Carmargue foals are born dark, but soon fade to white (gray).

OVERLEAF: A herd of Carmargues galloping through the salt marshes of the Rhône delta.

MUSTANG

The Mustang is a free-roaming horse of the American west. Although horses had once been present in North America, by the time the conquistadors arrived in the Americas in the 16th century, the indigenous prehistoric horses had long been extinct. The Spanish brought Iberian

horses with them in their ships, derived mainly from Arabs and Barbs. Many of these sleek, desert-bred, and resilient horses were allowed to wander off, spreading into North America and forming feral rather than wild herds. They became known as Mustangs.

Wild Mustangs of McCullough Peaks, Wyoming.

OPPOSITE: A lovely palomino Mustang.

Native American tribes came to value the Mustang's qualities and many were caught and domesticated by them. They even developed their own breeds based on the Mustang, such as the Appaloosa, the Cayuse Indian Pony, and the Chickasaw Indian Pony, also known as the Florida Cracker Horse.

There were between one- and two-million Mustangs in existence by the beginning of the 19th century, many of them still running free, though others had been caught and were being used by settlers. Unfortunately, the wild horses came to be regarded as pests, and were culled in their thousands to make way for cattle. It was not only the ranchers who were responsible for their decimation, thousands were also killed in the 20th century, sacrificed to the pet-food industry.

Sadly, there are fewer than 50,000 Mustangs in existence today, and in some areas numbers are dangerously low. Determined efforts are now being made to safeguard the breed for the future and, fortunately for the Mustang, the breed is now seen as an important part of the American heritage and a protected species.

Mustangs come in all colors, sizes, and builds, although horses that display Barb characteristics are particularly favored by breeders. The Mustang is easy to train, due to its innate intelligence, and it is tough and resilient. It can be any color, although it is mainly brown, chestnut, bay, or dun. Height varies from 14–16 hh.

> "You will hear the beat of a horse's feet,
> And the swish of a skirt in the dew,
> Steadily cantering through
> The misty solitudes,
> As though they perfectly knew
> The old lost road through the woods..."
> Rudyard Kipling

PRZEWALSKI'S HORSE

This is an ancient and wild breed, also known as the Mongolian or Asiatic Wild Horse. Primitive horses of this kind were hunted by man 20,000 years ago and the likenesses of similar horses can be seen in prehistoric cave paintings in Spain and France. The breed was almost certainly extinct in the wild, but recent introductions of herds has led to a new population. Genetically, it is the only true wild equine and the distant ancestor of the domestic horse.

The wild Przewalski's Horse cannot be domesticated, tamed, or ridden.

The earliest written evidence of its existence was in the 9th century, and it was mentioned again in 1226, when a herd of wild horses are supposed to have caused Ghengis Khan, the founder of the Mongol Empire, to fall from his horse.

Because of its isolation and the fierceness with which stallions protect their mares, the Mongolian horse's bloodline has remained pure and can be traced back to its primitive ancestors.

It gets its modern name from the man who brought it to the attention of the world, Colonel N. M. Przewalski, a Polish explorer who acquired the remains of a wild horse in 1881 from hunters who had discovered them in the Gobi Desert. He took them to the zoological museum in St. Petersburg, where naturalist I. S. Poliakoff examined them and decided that they belonged to a species of primitive wild horse. Following the discovery, some of the living horses were caught and kept in captivity in zoos and wildlife parks so that they would be saved from total extinction.

The captive population has increased rapidly and is carefully monitored at Prague Zoo, which holds the stud book of the breed. The horses are kept in conditions that are as natural as possible; some have been released back into the wild in China, Russia, and Mongolia, where they are a protected species, and a successful population can also be found in France.

The Przewalski is stocky and has an erect, dark-brown mane. The head is of medium size, with a broad forehead and a straight or slightly dished nose. The wild-looking eyes are set high on the head and are rather small. The nose tapers to a narrow muzzle with small, low-set nostrils. The body is strong, with a longish, straight back, a thick, short neck, and weak quarters. The legs are short and stocky with hard, tough hooves.

Przewalskis cannot be tamed and tend to be aggressive and ferocious, especially in the presence of their young. Being extremely hardy, they need very little extra attention.

Various shades of dun, ranging from yellow to red, are possible. Przewalskis have black manes and tails and black legs, often with zebra markings, and there is a black dorsal stripe running down the back. The muzzle and the area around the eyes is a creamy-white color. They range in height from 12–14 hh.

> "Far back, far back in our dark soul the horse prances... The horse, the horse! The symbol of surging potency and power of movement, of action in man!"
> D. H. Lawrence

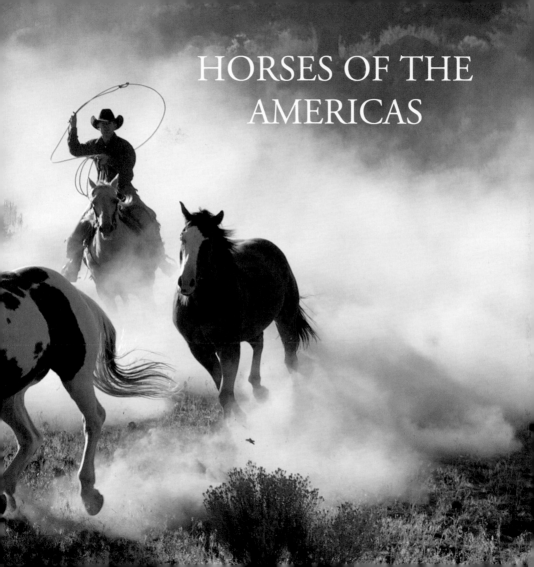

HORSES OF THE
AMERICAS

AMERICAN MINIATURE HORSE

This is not a pony but a scaled-down version of a horse; consequently it has all the characteristics of the larger animal. The first true miniature horses appeared in Europe in the 1600s, where they were bred as pampered pets for the nobility. Unfortunately, not all miniatures had such a good life and many were used as pit ponies in the coal mines of northern Europe, including the English Midlands. In the 1900s Lady Estella Hope continued the breeding program, and these are the lines that probably made their way to the United States.

Today the American Miniature Horse is stylish, well-proportioned, and the product of nearly 400 years of selective breeding. They make excellent all-rounders, especially in children's ridden classes such as show jumping and showing, and are also used for driving. The breed now has a closed stud book managed by the American Miniature Horse Association.

The American Miniature Horse should not exceed 34 inches (86cm) or 9 hh. It should have a similar conformation to a large, fine-boned horse such as a Thoroughbred or Warmblood. The overall impression should be of well-balanced symmetry, accompanied by strength, agility, and alertness; essentially, it should have all the appearance of the perfect horse in miniature.

The horse has a kind and affectionate nature. It is also gentle and placid, making it an ideal companion animal. It is excellent for children, and inspires confidence because it is easy to mount and willing to be ridden; its small stature also makes it suitable for the less physically able. The foals are particularly attractive, ranging from 16–21 inches (41–53cm) in height. They can be all colors and achieve no more than 9 hh in height.

The American Miniature is a friendly breed that interacts well with people and for this reason they are often kept as family pets.

44

AMERICAN SADDLEBRED

The origin of the American Saddlebred dates back to the 1600s, when horses were brought to America from Europe, and particularly from Britain and what is now the Irish Republic. They had been used for trotting and pacing, and their hardy constitutions and extravagant paces made them popular in their new home.

The Narragansett Pacer, which was developed in Rhode Island in the 17th century, is believed to have been an ancestor of these European horses, and it was the model on which all easy-gaited horses in America were based thereafter.

Now extinct, the Pacer was noted for its docility and easy motion, making long days in the saddle more comfortable for the rider in the early days of the American colonies. Narragansett mares and Thoroughbred stallions were allowed to mate, with the result that the pacing gait and all-round ability were transferred to their offspring. Eventually, they were known as the American Horse, and when combined with Morgan, Standardbred, and Thoroughbred blood, produced the American Saddlebred as it is known today.

While the traditional gaits of walk, trot, and canter are innate, the Saddlebred is a breed apart, having inherited the ability to add additional gaits to its repertoire. These include the slow gait or running walk, the stepping pace, and the slow rack, which is when both hooves on either side are in turn lifted almost simultaneously. This means that, at certain moments, all four hooves are off the ground, which is spectacular when combined with the horse's high-stepping action.

This high-stepping carriage is sometimes falsely encouraged by keeping the feet long and building the feet up, while in other cases, the muscles under the dock are nicked to produce an unnaturally stiff and high tail-carriage: these are illegal practices in most countries of the world. The use of the tail brace also persists. This is sometimes fitted to a stabled horse in order that a high tail-carriage can be preserved; this, however, is at the expense of the horse's comfort when it is at rest. This practice should be modified or preferably banished if true recognition is to be achieved within the broader equestrian world.

The Saddlebred has a commanding presence and subtle expression of movement. The head is small and narrow, carried high, and the alert and intelligent expression is accentuated by the horse's fine pricked ears. The eyes are gentle but intelligent and the nose is straight with slightly flared nostrils. The neck is long and elegant and also carried high. The withers are high and run neatly into the back, which is fairly long, as is the barrel-shaped body. The shoulders are narrower at the top than the bottom and slope to create the trademark fluid action. The tail-carriage is naturally high, joined to flat quarters flowing into strong and powerful loins.

The Saddlebred is biddable and easy to train. It is gentle and affectionate, loves people, and enjoys being handled. At the same time, it is spirited and proud, with a keen intelligence and an alert demeanor. It tends to become excitable under saddle.

Saddlebreds come in all the usual solid colors, including palomino and roan, and there is often a good deal of white on the head and legs. The coat, mane, and tail are fine and silky in texture. The horses typically range in size from 15–16.1 hh.

Saddlebreds are highly prized within the show ring, particularly in the harness and ridden classes in which they excel; but they are also capable of competing in other events, performing equally well as dressage horses and show jumpers.

APPALOOSA

For many centuries, spotted horses were highly prized in Europe and Asia and they were often featured in Chinese art. The Spanish conquistadors brought their own such horses with them on their travels, introducing the spotted gene to the Americas when they arrived. After a time, some of these horses passed to Native Americans, in particular the

The distinctive and spotted coats of three Appaloosas.

OPPOSITE: This handsome stallion has a blanket coat.

50

Nez Perce, who lived in north-eastern Oregon along the Palouse River. The Nez Perce, probably the first to introduce selective breeding, followed strict guidelines to produce the best results. They called this meeting of European and native stock the Appaloosa – possibly America's oldest breed.

Settlers eventually eliminated the Nez Perce, and the Appaloosa was dispersed throughout the land, the strain becoming weakened through random breeding. Nowadays the Appaloosa is enjoying renewed popularity. It does not have to be spotted, however, although it is mandatory that other criteria be present: the Appaloosa must have sclera around the eyeballs, striped hooves, and mottled skin beneath the hair.

The Appaloosa is a most versatile horse and looks good wearing Western tack. It is commonly

An Appaloosa spotted foal.

OPPOSITE: A red roan blanket with spots.

OVERLEAF: A blanket with spots.

used in Western events, such as roping, working cowhorse, and barrel-racing competitions. It is also used for showing, particularly in Britain, in riding horse and colored horse classes, and is proficient at cross-country and jumping.

There are some obvious differences between American and European Appaloosas. The U.S. types have been crossed with Quarter Horses, with the result that their size and conformation are similar. In Europe, Appaloosas are rather larger, nearer to the size of a warmblood, making them ideal for jumping and dressage purposes. The type is also becoming popular in the United States.

After the formation of the Appaloosa Horse Club in 1938, a more modern type developed with the addition of Arabian bloodlines, while the Quarter Horse element produced Appaloosas that performed better in sprint racing and in halter competition. In fact, many cutting and reining horses resulted from old-type Appaloosas crossed on Arabian bloodlines.

An infusion of Thoroughbred blood was added during the 1970s to produce horses more suited for racing. Many current breeders also attempt to breed away from the sparse, "rat tail" trait, with the result that modern Appaloosas have fuller manes and tails.

The Appaloosa is a workmanlike horse, with a fairly plain head and short, tapered ears. The eyes are alert and inquisitive, with the mandatory white rings or sclera around the eyeball rims. The neck and body are compact and well-muscled and the quarters are powerful with well-developed limbs. The tail and mane hair is relatively sparse. Hooves are often striped.

Appaloosas are great all-rounders: they are good-natured and hardy with plenty of stamina, speed, and agility.

Color patterns include Blanket, which is a solid

This Appaloosa is a blue roan blanket with spots.

white area, normally over the quarters and loins, with a contrasting base color; Spots, when white or dark spots cover all or a portion of the body; Blanket with Spots, when there is a white blanket with dark spots within the white area, usually in the same color as the base color; Roan, when a lighter-colored area develops on the face and over the back, loins, and quarters; Roan Blanket with Spots, when there is a roan blanket which has white and/or dark spots within the roan area; Solid, when a base color has no contrasting color in the form of an Appaloosa coat pattern. Appaloosas usually attain a height of between 14.2 and 15.2 hh.

> "A thousand horse and none to ride! –
> With flowing tail, and flying mane,
> Wide nostrils never stretched by pain,
> Mouths bloodless to the bit or rein,
> And feet that iron never shod,
> And flanks unscarred by spur or rod,
> A thousand horse, the wild, the free,
> Like waves that follow o'er the sea,
> Came thickly thundering on..."
>
> Lord Byron

FALABELLA

There is some evidence that the Falabella's ancestors were first seen in the 19th century, interspersed with the herds of South American Indians. But it was more probably the creation of the Falabella family, at their ranch near Buenos Aires in Argentina, over a century ago. The breed was established by first crossing small Arab and Thoroughbred stallions with Shetland Pony mares. Then, using selective breeding, it was made ever smaller.

The Falabella is one of the smallest horse breeds in the world.

The Falabella is not a pony: it is a miniature horse with all the conformation and character of a horse. Because of excessive in-breeding, however, the conformation of some individuals is far from ideal, consequently they tend to look rather odd. They are also weak for their size and can be ridden only by the smallest children. Today, breeders are attempting to rectify these faults and are generally trying to improve the breed.

LEFT and OVERLEAF: The Falabella, despite its size, is not considered a pony, but rather is a miniature horse.

Being affectionate, Falabellas make ideal pets and are sometimes allowed even into peoples' homes because of their small size. They are popular in special in-hand showing classes and are capable of pulling small carts.

Correctly bred, a Falabella should resemble a miniature Thoroughbred or Arab, though its Shetland ancestry may occasionally come to the fore. The head is refined and horse-like, with a straight nose and small, flared nostrils. The small ears are set wide apart, and the eyes are kind. The body is medium-length, with a slim frame, and the legs are fine, similar to those of a Thoroughbred.

The Falabella is a delightful breed. It provides all the pleasures of a larger breed but at a lower cost; this is particularly true as far as land requirements are concerned. Its constitution, however, is less than robust and it requires the same care that one would give to any finely bred horse. It is amenable, docile, and obedient.

Falabellas come in all solid colors, as well as gray and roan, and Appaloosa markings are also common. Ideally, they should stand no taller than 30 inches (76cm) from the ground.

MISSOURI FOX TROTTER

During the 19th century, settlers in Missouri and Arkansas developed the Missouri Fox Trotter. Initially, its purpose was to be a general riding horse, with the speed and endurance to cope with difficult terrain. The foundation stock for the breed was the Morgan, which was infused with Thoroughbred and Arab as well as Iberian blood.

As horses with elaborate gaits became more popular, the breed was later mated with the Saddlebred and Tennessee Walking Horse, which greatly improved its elegance, bearing and paces, including its foxtrot gait; this is basically a diagonal gait, like the trot, in which the horse appears to be walking with the front legs while trotting with the hind.

In the early days, the Fox Trotter had been a useful competitor in racing, but increasingly has reverted to its use as a general riding horse.

A stud book for the breed was eventually opened in 1948. The breed society, however, put in place strict guidelines that the Missouri Fox Trotter should have no artificial aids to influence and enhance its gait, such as nicking or setting the tail; consequently its action is not as pronounced or extravagant as that of the American Saddlebred, for example. The breed is popular in the United States, where it is used for general riding, showing, and endurance.

The head is a little plain, with a straight nose and a square muzzle with large open nostrils. The ears are medium-length and alert and the eyes have a kind but intelligent expression. The neck is medium-length and fairly well-developed, with prominent withers; the back is short, with strong loins and hindquarters. The tail is set fairly low, and the legs are long with large joints and well-shaped, strong hooves.

The Missouri Fox Trotter has a charming, easy-going manner. It is willing and obedient with excellent stamina and endurance. It comes in colors and can also be part-colored. Height is from 14–16 hh.

—m—

OVERLEAF: The Missouri Fox Trotter is a breed developed by settlers in the early 19th century. It quickly developed into a gaited breed appreciated for its stock horse abilities, stamina, and smooth gaits.

MORGAN

The Morgan is one of the earliest horse breeds developed in the United States. All Morgans can be traced back to just one stallion called Figure. Figure was later renamed Justin Morgan after its owner, Thomas Justin Morgan, a tavern keeper and singing teacher, who supplemented his income by breeding stallions.

The colt was born in around 1790 in Vermont. It is thought that its sire was probably a Welsh Cob, called True Briton, though little is known of the dam, other than that she may have had Oriental and Thoroughbred blood.

Morgans are strong, courageous, and hardworking. They have a sprited but tractable nature.

Thomas Justin Morgan was so impressed with his stallion's looks and personality that he eventually decided to put him to stud. The results were remarkable in that a foal the image of its father was always produced no matter what mare Justin Morgan covered. The sire's prowess as a marvelous harness and riding horse, moreover, seemed to be replicated in the offspring, the performance of each of them being second to none. In fact, all were amazed that such a significant and impressive breed could have developed from a single stallion.

Morgans are just as versatile today – used in harness competitions, shows, driving and trail-riding. The head should provide immediate evidence of quality, with beautiful and expressive eyes. The muzzle is small and the profile straight or slightly dished. The neck is well-crested and the shoulders strong. The hindquarters are large and strong and the legs sturdy.

A type known as the Park Morgan is bred particularly for its high-stepping action. Another type is the Pleasure Morgan, whose action is less exaggerated. All solid colors are acceptable in this breed. They stand somewhere between 14 and 15.2 hh.

PINTO/PAINT HORSE

The strikingly beautiful Pinto or Paint Horse (from the Spanish *pintado*, meaning "painted"), like many of the old American breeds, is descended from Iberian horses that were brought to the Americas by the conquistadors in the 16th century. They are sometimes referred to as "calico" horses in America.

In England and other Anglophone countries they are referred to as "piebalds" (black-and-white) or "skewbalds" (any other color and white) because their coats, of any solid color,

This Paint Horse is chestnut and white and looks very handsome in its Western tack.

OPPOSITE: The same horse at grass.

are heavily mottled with white; alternatively they are merely referred to as colored horses, though in the United States the Pinto is regarded as a separate breed.

The original Spanish horses were allowed to revert to a feral condition

and gradually extended into North America, where they roamed the Western deserts. Once domesticated by Native Americans, however, they became greatly revered; in fact, it was believed that the Pinto even possessed magic powers.

Ranchers also adopted these hardy horses, whose stamina and agility made them excellent for work over great distances. Today,

LEFT, OPPOSITE & OVERLEAF:
Beautifully marked examples.

they are still used as workhorses but also at rodeos; they are also used for trail-riding and showing and as all-round riding horses.

The Pinto has a fine head and graceful, well-defined neck. The ears are alert and of medium length, while the eyes indicate spirit and intelligence. They are usually quite short in the back, with long, strong legs, and hard, tough hooves. They are hardy and agile.

The Pinto is well-known for its striking coat, which can be black, chestnut, brown, bay, dun, sorrel, palomino, gray, or roan, patched with large areas of white. There are three distinctive types of coat pattern: Tobiano, in which the head is like that of any solid-colored horse, but there are round or oval spots resembling shields running over the neck and chest. One or both flanks may be colored white or a color can predominate, while the tail is often bi-colored; Overo, which is predominantly dark or white, though the white shouldn't cross the back between withers and tail. The head should be white with scattered irregular markings on the rest of the body. At least one leg should be dark and the tail is usually one color; Tovero is a mixture of the two. Pintos stand between 14.2 and 15.2 hh.

PASO FINO

Originating in Puerto Rico, the foundation of the Paso Fino is old Spanish or Iberian stock. It has the same bloodlines, inherited from horses brought to the Americas by the Spanish conquistadors in the 16th century; in terms of character and conformation, however, different environments have caused slight variations in their evolution.

LEFT, OPPOSITE & OVERLEAF: The Paso Fino is a naturally gaited horse breed dating back to a time when horses were imported to the Caribbean from Spain.

The Paso Fino is a naturally gaited horse, like the Peruvian Paso or Stepping Horse and another lesser-known Colombian breed, and although it is predominantly a working horse, these attributes make it stand out from the crowd. Aficionados claim that because of its natural, even, four-beat gait, that can be performed at varying speeds, it is the smoothest riding horse in the world. The classic *fino* is a collected gait, executed with a rapid footfall that covers little ground. The *paso corto* is a moderate gait, useful in trail riding, and the *paso largo* is a fast gait in which the horse can reach speeds equivalent to a canter or slow gallop. Not all Paso Finos can perform the classic *fino*, but the majority perform the other gaits with ease.

There are another two variants: the *sobre paso*, a more natural gait in which the horse is allowed a loose rein and is relaxed, and which is used in general riding rather than the show ring; and the *andadura*, which is a fast, pacing gait. This is uncomfortable, however, so it is only performed for short periods. The rest of the time the horse's effortless gait makes riding it extremely comfortable and smooth.

Paso Finos are in great demand for showing and displays. The head is fine, almost Arab-like, with a straight nose and flaring nostrils. It has longish, well-shaped ears and intelligent eyes. The body is very Spanish, similar to the Andalusian's, with a good sloping shoulder, well-developed neck, and a medium-length back. It has slightly sloping quarters and a low-set tail. The legs are sturdy and strong with large hocks.

The Paso Fino has an excellent temperament and great enthusiasm. Despite its small stature it is very strong; in fact, even the smallest will easily carry a man over hills and rough terrain. It may be any color and stands between 14 and 15 hh.

PERUVIAN PASO

Known for its smooth ride, the Peruvian Paso, or Peruvian Stepping Horse, as the name suggests orginates in Peru. It shares much of its descent with the Paso Fino, the national horse of Puerto Rico, the foundation of both breeds being Barb and old Spanish or Iberian stock brought to the Americas by the conquistadors in the 16th century.

LEFT, OPPOSITE & OVERLEAF:
The Peruvian Paso is distinguished by its three distinctive gaits that are passed from mare to foal.

The Peruvian Paso has adapted well to its environment and is able to carry riders great distances over dangerous mountain terrain with safety and comfort. It has also adapted to the high altitudes of the Andes Range and has a larger, stronger heart, and greater lung capacity than other breeds; this enables it to function energetically at heights where oxygen is scarce.

Like the other Paso breeds, the Peruvian has the natural ability to

perform the attractive four-beat lateral gaits that make riding long distances so comfortable for the rider without tiring the horse. There are three gaits: the *paso corto*, used for practical purposes; the *paso fino*, an exaggerated slow

LEFT: A Peruvian Paso tacked up in a traditional bridle.

OPPOSITE: Two yearlings.

OVERLEAF: A Peruvian Paso stallion.

gait used in the show ring and in parades, which has the appearance almost of slow motion; and the *paso largo*, which is fast. These traits are passed from mare to foal and are completely natural, needing no artificial aids. Once a person becomes accustomed to the gaits (the horse never trots or gallops) the Peruvian makes an excellent riding horse.

In stature, the Peruvian is similar to its cousin the Paso Fino. The head is fine and resembles that of the Barb, with shapely pricked ears and a proud, alert look. The nostrils are readily dilated, presumably to allow as much oxygen as possible to be taken in. The body has all the evidence of a Spanish inheritance and is similar to the Andalusian's. The legs are sturdy, quite long, and well-muscled with hard hooves.

While the Peruvian Paso is hardy and energetic, it is also even-tempered and intelligent. It is an obedient and willing worker. Peruvians may be any color, but bay or chestnut, with white on the head and legs, is permitted. The mane and tail are abundant, with fine, lustrous hair that may be straight or curly. They range in height between 14 and 15.2 hh.

—⋙—

PONY OF THE AMERICAS

The Pony of the Americas is a relatively new breed dating from the 1950s and is the result of an accidental cross between a Scottish Shetland Pony and an Appaloosa mare with Arab connections. When the foal, Black Hand I, was born, it was found to be a smaller version of its dam and it was this stallion that became the foundation of America's first pony breed.

LEFT, OPPOSITE & OVERLEAF:
The Pony of the Americas is a breed known for its kindness, gentle disposition, and intelligence.

The breed has the appearance of a small horse rather than a pony; later on, further refinement was added when Quarter Horse and Arab bloodlines were introduced, producing the showy, high-stepping action so popular in the show ring today.

Similar in stature to British Thoroughbred ponies, the Pony of the Americas is ideal for small children, who find it easy to handle. It is also strong enough to carry a small adult and is used in endurance, trail-riding and show jumping, as well as trotting and pony flat-racing.

The head is very Arab, with a broad forehead, small pricked ears, and a straight or slightly dished nose. The eyes are large and kind. The body is of medium length, with a good sloping shoulder, well-developed quarters, and fine but strong legs. It is strong and hardy, with a calm but willing disposition. It shares similar markings with the Appaloosa, and stands between 11.2 and 14 hh.

—w—

"He knows when you're happy
He knows when you're comfortable
He knows when you're confident
And he always knows when you have carrots."
Anonymous

QUARTER HORSE

It is no surprise that the Quarter Horse holds pride of place in the hearts of all American horse-lovers, seeing that it was the first breed to become established in the United States.

The Quarter Horse's origins can be traced back 500 years to the time when the Spanish conquistadors brought Iberian and Oriental horses to Florida. English colonists eventually acquired these horses from

LEFT & OPPOSITE: The Quarter Horse is an American breed that excels at sprinting short distances.

Chickasaw Indians, which they crossed with their own English horses, mainly Thoroughbreds, then refined them again with more Thoroughbred blood.

Before the days of race tracks, the early colonists used to race their horses down the main street, which was usually about a quarter-of-a-mile long. The name Quarter Horse, therefore, came from the ability of these horses to achieve great speeds over a short distance. The powerful hindquarters of the Quarter Horse gave it great acceleration and even today it is faster than the Thoroughbred over short sprints.

Not only was the Quarter Horse a talented sprinter, it also made a good riding horse, pulled wagons, and was an efficient packhorse. Its most valuable attribute, however, was its natural instinct to round up herds. This undoubtedly had been inherited from its Iberian forebears, which had nerves of steel and amazing agility. They also had plenty of cow sense, having worked the bullrings of Portugal and Spain for generations. Today, racing predominates, but their use in rodeos, trailing, and as all-round family mounts is widespread across the United States, Canada, Australia, and even parts of Europe.

Quarter Horses can be quite large animals, due to the influence of the Thoroughbred in their breeding. The head is relatively small and the eyes are

bright and set far apart. The neck, hindquarters, and back are extremely muscular, which makes the feet appear relatively small.

Quarter Horses are easy to maintain, and are enthusiastic, honest, and energetic. Their coats may be of any color, and their height range is between 14.2 and 16 hh.

LEFT & OPPOSITE: The Quarter Horse excels on the racetrack but also makes a good all-rounder.

TENNESSEE WALKING HORSE

A breed of gaited horse, the Tennessee (or Plantation) Walking Horse originated in the Deep South of the United States and was recognized as the ideal utility breed to carry plantation owners around their large estates. The smooth, gliding gait of the "Walker" (as the breed is also known) provided hours of comfort in the saddle; the

LEFT, OPPOSITE & OVERLEAF:
The Tennessee Walking Horse or Tennessee Walker is a breed known for its unique gaits and flashy movement.

movement is performed from the elbow rather than the shoulder, thus transmitting the minimum of movement to the rider. Although still widely ridden for pleasure, the Walker is nowadays extensively bred for the show ring, and it is also used as a general riding and harness horse.

In fact there are two or three characteristic gaits, the flat-footed walk,

the running walk, and the canter. The first horse perceived to have this natural talent was foaled in 1837, but it took another 50 years or so to establish the breed as it is today.

The Thoroughbred, Standardbred, American Saddlebred, Narragansett Pacer, and Morgan bloodlines all played their part in establishing this distinctive breed, but it was one stallion, born in 1886, that became its foundation stallion. It possessed all the desired qualities, such as the delightful temperament and the characteristic gaits. Most of the offspring inherited their sire's traits and he subsequently enjoyed many successful years at stud. Once a breed association had become established, approximately 300,000 horses were registered.

The Walker has a large head with a straight profile, gentle eyes, and pointed ears. The neck is arched and muscular, with a broad base that enables the head to be carried elegantly high. The breed has plenty of bone, which adds to its sturdiness, and a short-coupled and level topline. The limb joints are well-made, with particularly powerful hocks that allow the hindlegs to step well under the body. The tail, which is usually left long, is often nicked and set artificially high.

Walkers are naturally gentle and calm, but it is their unusual gaits for which they are most famous. Although the gaits are inherited, they need to be developed by further training. The flat walk, running walk, and canter are natural to the breed. The running walk has several variations: the rack, the stepping pace, the fox-trot, and single-foot.

Tennessee Walking Horses may be any color, but especially black, chestnut, brown, gray, roan, or bay. Height is between 15 and 17 hh.

HORSES OF WESTERN EUROPE

ANDALUSIAN

This revered and important Spanish breed is one of the oldest to have been handled and ridden by man: there is further evidence of this fact in cave paintings, which confirm that horses of this kind were present in the Iberian Peninsula in around 5000 BC.

The Andalusian's lineage stems from the Sorraia Pony, which still exists in Iberia, and

LEFT, OPPOSITE & OVERLEAF: Throughout its history, the Andalusian has been known for its prowess as a warhorse, and was prized by the nobility.

the North African Barb, with additional Arab and Oriental strains. It evolved in Iberia, most of which was then known as Andalusia, at the time of the Moorish occupation of 711. The result was a horse with a head-carriage that was high and proud, and paces that were extravagant and highly placed.

The Andalusian was particularly valued as a warhorse, having all the qualities that enabled it to perform well in battle. (It is interesting to note that El Cid's mount, Babieca, was an Andalusian.) Later, in the 16th century, the conquistadors brought the horse with them to the Americas, where it became the basis of all American breeds, which also share lineage with the Lusitano, Carthusian, and Altér Real.

The Andalusian bloodline is evident in around 80 percent of modern breeds and has had a particular influence on the Connemara, native to Ireland, the Lipizzaner of the Balkans, and the Cleveland Bay, and Welsh Cob of the British Isles. However, its popularity was not to last, and in around 1700 the Andalusian's heavy, robust conformation fell from favor, when lighter, sleeker animals, used for hunting and racing, became more fashionable. Andalusians suffered even more when a plague and famine almost wiped them out; a few survived in the Carthusian monasteries of Castello, Jerez, and Seville, where breeding from the best of the animals continued.

Today, the Andalusian can still be traced back to these lines, the purest and most beautiful of which are still referred to as *caballos Cartujanos*. Their extreme rarity forced the Spanish government to ban their export for over 100 years, but the embargo was lifted in the 1960s, and they now enjoy popularity around the world.

Today, the Andalusian is used for bullfighting and display riding, where its power and agility allow it to execute the intricate movements with ease. They excel

The Andalusian Horse Association only accepts gray, bay, and black. This stallion is dark bay.

at advanced classical dressage and at show jumping and are also useful for general riding and driving. They are often to be seen in hand in the show ring.

These muscular horses have great presence and beauty. The neck is heavy, with a well-developed crest. The mane is abundant and should be kept long. The head-carriage is noble and high, the forehead wide with expressive, medium-length ears. The eyes are dark-brown and gentle, the nostrils are flared, and the jaw is large and well-muscled. The withers are well-rounded and the shoulder is long and sloping. The chest is broad, the croup rounded, and the low-set tail is thick and long. The body is rounded and short-coupled, adding to the overall strength. The legs are strong with large joints and the hooves are rounded and compact.

The Andalusian is famous for its extravagant paces. Movement is elevated and extended, making the horse look as if it were floating on air. All paces are smooth, showy, and spectacular.

Andalusians are proud and courageous, and although spirited to ride, they have amiable temperaments. They have soft mouths, making them extremely obedient when ridden correctly.

Gray and bay coats are most in evidence, but others are accepted by the Andalusian Horse Association. In Spain, according to the studbook, only gray, bay, and black are acceptable. Height is between 15 and 16.2 hh.

ANGLO-ARAB

The Anglo-Arab is technically a crossbreed that derives its name from two of the world's greatest breeds, the Thoroughbred, which is of English (Anglo) origin, and the Arab. The rules of Anglo-Arab breeding in the United Kingdom are very strict, and only these two bloodlines can be present. Other countries have their own rules, with some adding elements of their own native breeds, the French Anglo-Arab being one.

There are other stipulations, however, and at least 25 percent Arab content is the norm.

Because the Anglo-Arab is a mixture of two breeds it is not actually recognized as such, with one exception: the fore-mentioned French Anglo-Arab. There are other variations which appear all over Europe, the

The Anglo-Arab is an exciting blend of Thoroughbred and Arab that combines the qualities of both breeds.

Gidrán or Hungarian Anglo-Arab, the Shagya Arab, also from Hungary, the Russian Strelets-Arab, and Spain's Hispano-Arab.

Anglo-Arabs make superb riding horses and excel in most disciplines, including show jumping, eventing, and dressage. They also do well in riding-horse showing classes, where, unlike the pure Arab, which must be left as it is, their manes and tails can be plaited. The combination of the Thoroughbred's complaisant nature and the strength, stamina, and intelligence of the Arab make an ideal combination.

The interesting thing about breeding Anglo-Arabs is that one never knows how they are going to turn out: they can be either predominantly Arab or Thoroughbred, or a combination of both; either way they are ideal all-rounders and extremely rewarding to ride.

The Anglo-Arab should have the skeletal structure and conformation of the Thoroughbred and the tail and head-carriage of the Arab, though this can occasionally vary, with some having lighter bones than others. The head should have unmistakable Arab features, with a dished or straight profile that is not quite as extreme as the Arab's. The eyes should indicate that the horse can be spirited on occasions, while the nostrils are large and flared. The ears are medium-sized, fine, pointed, and expressive. The head-carriage is fairly high, with a well-developed crest. The Anglo-Arab should have the good sloping shoulders, deep chest, and powerful hindquarters of the Thoroughbred. The tail-carriage can be either high like the Arab's or lower as in the Thoroughbred.

Anglo-Arabs are usually affectionate and intelligent. They are also brave and spirited and will always give their very best. The most usual colors are brown, bay, chestnut, and gray, while black is rather more rare. There is often white on the face and legs, but never on the rest of the body. Anglo-Arabs stand somewhere between 14.2 and 16.1 hh.

CONNEMARA

The Connemara pony is a breed native to Ireland, although it is not indigenous to the country. It is thought that it was brought to Ireland 2,500 years ago when the Celts settled in Ireland and brought their ponies with them. The Celts were traders and traveled to and from Mediterranean ports, which makes it likely that their ponies were of Oriental descent,

LEFT, RIGHT & OVERLEAF: Semi-wild Connemara ponies can still be seen, peacefully grazing in their native rugged terrain.

probably Barb. In medieval times these horses were bred with the Irish Hobeye, which was a much coveted riding horse, famous for its speed, agility, and endurance.

Legend has it that further blood was added to the breed when the

Spanish Armada sank off the coast of Ireland and Iberian horses swam ashore and mated with native breeds. Later, the breed was further improved with infusions of Hackney, Welsh Cob, Irish Draft, Clydesdale, and Thoroughbred bloodlines.

The Connemara derives its name from the region of that name, which included Connaught and Galway a few hundred years ago. The terrain is rocky and mountainous with very little vegetation. The weather can be atrocious with piercing winds and driving rain coming in from the Atlantic. Consequently, the Connemara has evolved into an extremely hardy specimen which is sure-footed and agile and has extraordinary jumping abilities.

Historically, it was used as a draft animal, transporting peat and seaweed as well as taking potatoes and corn to market. Nowadays it is used for hunting, eventing, show jumping, and driving; it is often crossed with the Thoroughbred to produce an excellent jumping horse.

The Connemara is a riding pony of excellent quality. The head is fine and set quite high, with small pricked ears, clever eyes, and a straight nose with fairly large nostrils. The neck is of medium length and well-muscled and the shoulders are sloping; it has a deep girth, a straight back, and well-developed quarters. The legs are short but elegant and strong, with very hard hooves. Intelligent animals, they have a calm and kindly disposition. Connemaras are excellent all-rounders and being hardy are easy to maintain. They are most commonly gray, but bay, black, dun, and brown are also possible. They stand between 13 and 14.2 hh.

—ww—

"A horse is worth more than riches."
Spanish proverb

DARTMOOR

The Dartmoor pony has inhabited the moors of Devon in the south-west of England as early as 2000 BC, a fact confirmed by remains excavated on Shaugh Moor. The earliest written reference to the Dartmoor is in the will of Awlfold of Crediton, who died in 1012. The breed stems from the Celtic Pony which went on to breed with other British natives;

LEFT, RIGHT & OVERLEAF: Now allowed to roam free, Dartmoor ponies were once used for carrying heavy loads of tin across the moors.

later, there were additions of Roadster, Welsh Pony, Cob, Arab, and in recent times, Thoroughbred.

The Dartmoor pony comes from the county of Devon in the south-west of England and gets its name from the area of wild moorland which it still roams. Standing over 1,000 feet (305m) above sea level, with wind and rain driving off the sea, it is at times an inhospitable place, with rocky outcrops and sparse vegetation. Consequently, the pony is extremely hardy and sure-footed and has plenty of stamina.

Dartmoors fail to thrive if left solely to their own devices, however, and require extra hay in winter, which farmers put out for them. This was confirmed during the Second World War when Dartmoor was completely out of bounds. As a result, the population dwindled to only two stallions and 12 mares because of the lack of supplementary feeding. Nowadays the breed has been greatly improved and with careful monitoring is now flourishing. Children like to ride Dartmoors and they are also used for showing and driving.

The Dartmoor has a small, nicely-set neat head, with small, alert ears, and an intelligent and kindly eye. The neck is of medium length and fairly well-developed, as are the back, loins, and quarters. The tail is high-set, the legs are shapely but sturdy, and the hooves are well-formed and hard.

Dartmoors make excellent children's ponies, and their small size makes them easily manageable. They also have kind and docile natures.

The Dartmoor's most striking feature is that it moves with almost no knee flexion: this produces a long, free-flowing stride similar to that of a horse and is very comfortable for the rider. Dartmoors are mainly bay and brown with only a little white on the legs and face. Height is up to 12.2 hh.

EXMOOR

The Exmoor is said to have existed since the Ice Age, so is truly ancient. Exmoor's isolated position, covering remote areas of the counties of Devon and Somerset in England, has ensured that very little cross-breeding has occurred, which has maintained the purity of the breed; indeed, the Exmoor pony is one of the purest breeds in the world, unlike its near

LEFT, RIGHT & OVERLEAF: The *Domesday Book* records ponies on Exmoor in 1086, and descendants of ponies removed from the moor in 1818 form the foundation bloodstock of today's Exmoor breed.

cousin, the Dartmoor, which, having been more accessible to other influences, has been subjected to more evolutions. Exmoors are truly wild ponies and they still live up on the moors. Being regarded as a rare breed, with only 1,000 ponies worldwide, they are now closely monitored. There are aproximately 300 breeding mares in the U.K., producing around 130 foals a year. Half of these mares still live on Exmoor and to protect the purity of the breed each foal is inspected, numbered, and branded with the society's mark on the flank and the herd number on the shoulder.

Various farms in the area are involved in the breeding of the Exmoor ponies, with the result that their future is now much brighter. Nowadays, Exmoors are also being bred in other parts of Britain, but the moors ponies are still used as foundation stock to ensure the purity of the breed.

The Exmoor's head is large, with a broad forehead and hooded eyes (known as "toad-eyes") to protect them from the elements. The ears are thick and short and the nose is straight. The neck is also thick and well-developed, with a deep chest; the short, fine legs are nevertheless muscular, with a little feathering around the fetlocks. The hooves are small and hard. The coat is dense with a thick, wiry mane and tail.

Exmoors are extremely tough and can live out all-year-round. If they are to be domesticated, they must be caught and broken in while young. They are good-natured, willing, and obedient and make good children's ponies.

Exmoors can be bay, brown, or dun with black points. There should be no white, but the distinctive mealy markings should be present around the eyes, muzzle, and flanks. Mares should not exceed 12.2 hh or stallions 12.3 hh.

FELL

A versatile mountain and moreland breed, the Fell is closely related to the Dales Pony, though it originated on the western side of the Pennines, inhabiting the hills and mountains of Cumbria in north-eastern England. It is a descendant of the Celtic Pony, that once roamed much of northern Europe, and which the Romans used as draft animals and in raids against the Picts. They

LEFT: Fell ponies are usually black but can be gray, brown, or bay.

OVERLEAF: A smart black Fell stallion.

were later used by reivers – the cattle-raiders of the Scottish Border country – because they were known to be sure-footed and with plenty of stamina.

The Fell's checkered history became more eventful when they were used by smugglers around Britain's northern coast. They were also bred by Cistercian monks, who introduced gray ponies to signify that they belonged to the monastery.

Over the years, and like the Dales, the breed was improved by mating with other stock, such as the Friesian, to which the Fell bears a resemblance. It remains much purer then the Dales, however, which has been subjected to rather more added bloodstock.

Like many native breeds, numbers declined during and after the two world wars, when farms switched to machinery and motorized transport as they became more readily available. The Fell, however, remained popular as a riding and driving pony and its fortunes have been happily reversed. Today, the Fell is an all-round family pony, strong enough to carry an adult and docile enough for children to ride. They make excellent trekking ponies, making them popular with the tourist industry. They are also used in harness and are still occasionally used to herd sheep.

The Fell bears a strong resemblance to the Friesian. The head is noble, with a broad forehead and a straight or slightly dished, tapering nose, with large flaring nostrils. The eyes are proud and intelligent and the ears small and neat. The head sits well on the neck, which is of medium length, strong but not overdeveloped. The shoulders are well-muscled and sloping, ensuring a good smooth action. The body is sturdy with a strong back and deep chest. The legs are strong and muscular, with fine feathering present on the backs of the legs; the hooves are well-shaped and are the characteristic blue color. Mane and tail should not be trimmed but left to grow naturally.

The Fell Pony has an excellent constitution and like most mountain and moorland ponies it is hardy and able to live out all-year-round. It is easy-going and enjoys the company of humans beings; it is a free spirit, however, and can be willful on occasions. Fell Ponies are famous for their excellent paces, which make them comfortable to ride. They excel at endurance events and are fast in the bargain, which is an asset in harness.

Fells are usually pure black with no white markings, but bay, gray, and brown are also possible. A small amount of white is permissable around the fetlocks or in the form of a small star on the forehead. They stand around 14 hh.

—⁓—

FJORD

The distinctive Norwegian Fjord is most likely descended from the Przewalski or Asiatic Wild Horse, which in turn was descended from Ice Age horses. It seems to have retained many of its ancestors' characteristics, including the pale coat, the dorsal stripe down the back, and the occasional zebra stripes on the legs, which were typical of the ancient breed.

LEFT, OPPOSITE & OVERLEAF: In their homeland of Norway, Fjords are bred under government control, and only champion stock can be exported.

The primitive breed was improved over many hundreds of years by breeding with the Celtic Pony and Tarpan. The result has been utilized for thousands of years, and there is evidence of its use in raids and battles from Viking artifacts. The Vikings had a particularly bloodthirsty approach to selection: they allowed stallions to fight to the death, ensuring that the stronger specimens continued the breed.

Fjords still have their manes clipped in the manner seen on Viking rune stones; the mane is unusual in that the hair is cream on the outer edges and black in the center, being a part of the dorsal stripe. The mane is therefore clipped so that the black part remains prominent.

The Fjord has been used to improve many other Northern European breeds, including the Icelandic and Highland. Today they can be seen over most of Scandinavia, mainly as children's riding ponies. The Fjord is sure-footed and excellent at trekking and long-distance endurance events. It is also popular in harness, where it has been successful in competition. Some are still used around the farm for light plowing and as packhorses.

The Fjord has an attractive head: it is short and wide with short, neat ears, a slightly dished face and large nostrils. The eyes are large and kind, and the neck is short and thick, accentuated by the traditionally clipped mane. The body is sturdy, with sloping quarters and a low-set tail. The legs are strong with plenty of bone and the feet are tough and hard.

All Fjords are dun-colored, which is a body color that is a tan, gold, or a related shade with darker (usually black or dark brown) points and primitive markings. White markings are discouraged, though a small star is acceptable. Some also have zebra stripes on the legs. The hooves are most often dark, but can be a lighter brown color on lighter-colored horses. Fjords stand between 13.2 and 14.2 hh.

FRIESIAN

The Friesian descended from a native breed that once roamed Friesland – the western part of the ancient region of Frisia – 3,000 years ago, and where the remains of a similar coldblooded horse have been found. As riding horses, the Friesian's history is an ancient one, with evidence that it was used by Roman soldiers when they were building Hadrian's Wall in around AD 150; this is supported

LEFT, OPPOSITE & OVERLEAF:
The Friesian horse is known for its luxurious long mane and tail. When prepared for the the show ring, the tail is allowed to reach the ground.

by the fact that Fell and Dales breeds, native to the English Pennines, are also descended from Friesian stock. Friesian bloodlines are also present in the Orlov Trotter and in most American trotters.

Over the years, the original, rather heavy and plain breed was infused with Oriental and Andalusian blood; this improved the breed to such an extent that during the 17th century, Friesians could be seen performing haute école alongside Spanish horses, and Friesians were in demand as elegant carriage horses. During the 19th century, however, the Friesian became something of a rarity, being almost exclusively restricted to Friesland, where it was used as a general riding horse and trotter. By the end of the First World War, the Friesian was in dire peril of extinction, with only three stallions and a few mares still in existence. Fortunately, with careful breeding and an infusion of Oldenburg blood, the Friesian is once again flourishing; today, it is in evidence all over the world – admired for its noble presence and expressive trot, which is particularly striking in harness. It is still used in haute école disciplines.

From the latter part of the 20th century until the present, demand for purebred Friesians, particularly the "modern," finer-boned, taller, more agile version of the breed, increased, so breeders have produced both purebreds and a lighter-weight crossbred horse with valued characteristics, resulting in the Friesian cross and the Friesian Sporthorse.

The head is proud and of medium size, with small, alert ears pointing slightly inward. The eyes are kindly and expressive, the head-carriage is high and elegant, and the neck is of medium length with a high crest. The withers are well-developed, tapering into the back muscles, and the shoulders sloping. The back is of medium length, strong and straight, leading to well-developed loins and quarters. The legs are clean and strong with slight feathering, and the mane and tail are long and luxuriant; when showing, mane and tail should be left untrimmed. The Friesian has a proud bearing and is gentle and amenable if rather energetic. It is always black, and only the smallest of stars is permitted on the forehead. Usually Friesians stand around 15–15.2 hh, but some Friesians have been bred larger, reaching more than 16 hh.

LEFT & OPPOSITE: The Friesian breed is most often recognized by its black coat color; what makes it unusual is that it rarely has any white markings on it at all, with only a small star being permitted.

GYPSY VANNER

The origins of the Gypsy Vanner (or Cob or Drummer Horse) lie with the Irish Travelers, or Gypsies, of the British Isles. The relationship between Gypsies and horses goes back hundreds of years, but it was only some 50 years ago that the horse came to be regarded as a special breed. Until recently, the Irish Cob or traditional colored cob was

LEFT, OPPOSITE & OVERLEAF:
Originally bred by the Gypsies of the British Isles, the Gypsy Vanner is recognizable by its long, flowing mane and tail and the profusion of feathers on its legs.

considered to be more of a type than a breed, until finally, in 1996, it was recognized and registered as such.

Crossed with Friesian, Shire, Dales Pony, and Clydesdale, it is now a heavy horse, variable in size and appearance.

The Gypsy Vanner's build is powerful and compact. It should have a "sweet head," meaning that the head is in proportion with the rest of the body. It has an abundant mane and plenty of feathering. The chest should be broad and the withers rounded; the knees should be large and flat and the hooves substantial.

Although known for its extreme docility, the horse is also intelligent and athletic; it must be sound enough, both mentally and physically, to endure a lifetime on the road. It comes in all colors, including piebald and skewbald, and stands between 14 and 15.2 hh.

—⁓—

"Gipsy gold does not chink and glitter. It gleams in the sun and neighs in the dark."
Attributed to the
Claddaugh Gypsies of Galway, Ireland

HAFLINGER

It is thought that the Haflinger comes from the South Tyrol in Austria, close to its border with Italy; borders have changed many times throughout history, however, making the exact location impossible to pinpoint. The Haflinger is not unlike the slightly larger Italian Avelignese, and the two probably had common ancestors.

LEFT, OPPOSITE & OVERLEAF:
The attractive, versatile Haflinger is fast becoming popular in North America. The primary objective of the American Haflinger Registry is to keep the breed pure.

The Haflinger may have been the result of native stock breeding with Oriental horses, which were left behind when the Ostrogoths were driven north by the Byzantine forces in the 6th century AD. Another story is that King Louis IV of Germany gave a Burgundian stallion to his son as a wedding gift, which was mated with local mares of Oriental origin to produce the Haflinger breed; either way it would seem that Oriental bloodlines are present.

What is known for sure, however, is that the modern Haflinger breed was improved in 1868 when the Arab stallion, El-Bedavi XXII, was imported to the region and bred with Haflinger mares; today, all Haflingers are related to this one stallion.

Today the Haflinger is still to be found in Austria, where it is closely monitored, not only in government-organized breeding programs but also by private individuals. The breed is popular the world over, particularly in Europe, where it is used in the forests and farms of the Tyrol. It is also useful in harness, and as a children's riding pony and family pet.

The Arab influence can be clearly seen in the Haflinger's fine head, which presents a sharp contrast to the stocky body. The nose is slightly dished and the eyes are large and attentive. The ears are small and alert and the nostrils and muzzle neat. The neck is well-proportioned, with fine sloping shoulders, good withers, and a deep girth. The body is broad and strong, with muscular quarters and a high-set tail. Legs are of medium length with tough hooves.

The Haflinger has rhythmic, ground-covering gaits. The walk is relaxed but energetic, and the trot and canter are elastic, energetic, and athletic with a natural tendency to be light on the forehand and balanced. There is some knee action, and the canter has a very distinct motion forward and upward.

The Haflinger is a sociable animal and enjoys the company of people. It is intelligent, trustworthy, and docile, making it an excellent work pony and safe with children. Haflingers are hardy and require only moderate feeding; but they do require shelter from cold winds and wet weather. Their most striking feature is their flaxen mane and tail that are usually left long.

Various shades of chestnut, liver, or red are permitted, sometimes with a little dappling over paler areas. Height is around 14 hh.

—⧉—

HANOVERIAN

Hanoverians owe their evolution to warfare, and by the Middle Ages had developed into large, cobby horses, capable of carrying a knight clad in full armor. The type was favored for many centuries until changes in warfare techniques meant that a lighter horse was eventually required. At this time, the Hanoverian was still a heavy breed, even though it was somewhat taller and more agile than a cob. By the 17th century, three distinctive types were being bred for military purposes: Hanoverian, Mecklenburg, and Danish horses.

But it was in the 18th century that the Hanoverian truly came into its own, when a member of the House of Hanover, in

LEFT, OPPOSITE & OVERLEAF: The Hanoverian is one of the oldest and most successful of the warmbloods, excelling in show jumping, dressage, and eventing.

148

the person of George I, ascended the British throne in 1714. He spent much of his reign in Hanover, however, and for the next 100 years or so the Hanoverian was nurtured and improved. English Thoroughbred stallions were bred with Hanoverian mares, and Cleveland Bay bloodlines were also added to produce a horse that was still relatively heavy but also suitable for farm use and coachwork.

It was George II who established the state stud at Celle in 1735, where horses for agriculture, riding, and driving were bred. Here the Hanoverian

breed was improved still further, with additions of Trakehner and Thoroughbred blood; the Hanoverian breed registry was founded in 1888. This horse was very similar to today's famous competition horse.

Probably the best known of all the warmbloods, the modern Hanoverian excels in top dressage and show jumping the world over. Nowadays, the Society of Breeders of the Hanoverian Warmblood Horse is responsible for the purity of the breed. Approximately 160 Hanoverians, mostly stallions, are kept by the state and based at Celle, where they are subjected to tests that assess soundness, conformation, and character for several months before they are allowed to mate.

The Hanoverian has played a large part in the improvement and formation of other warmblood breeds, such as Westphalian, Mecklenburg, and Brandenburg horses. Hanoverians now come in two types: the heavier horses are used for show jumping, while the lighter ones, which have more of the Thoroughbred in their make-up, are used for dressage.

The Hanoverian is near-perfect in conformation and its Thoroughbred characteristics are immediately discernible. The head is of medium size, with a straight nose and keen, alert eyes, and pricked ears. The neck has a graceful arch and is long and muscular, while the chest is well-developed with a deep girth and sloping shoulder. The back is of medium length, with muscular loins and powerful quarters. The legs are strong with large joints, ending in well-shaped hooves.

The most important feature of the Hanoverian, and one of the crucial tests that stallions have to undergo at Celle, is one of character: only horses with an even temperament and a willing disposition are allowed to breed. Hanoverians are noble and proud, with an excellent free-flowing action which allows them to excel at advanced dressage. They come in all solid colors, often with white on the face and legs. They range in height from 15.2–17 hh.

"Let us ride together, blowing mane and hair,
Careless of the weather, miles ahead of care,
ring of hoof and snaffle, swing of waist and
hip, trotting down the twisted road with the
world let slip."

Anonymous

HOLSTEIN

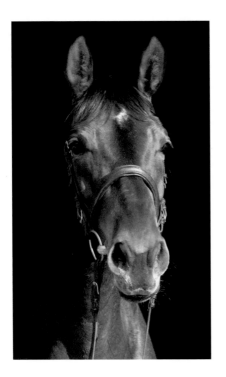

The Holstein breed dates to the 13th century, when Gerhard I, Count of Holstein and Storman, permitted the monks of the Uetersen monastery to graze their quality horses, which they bred themselves, on private land. These were native stock that had been mixed with Andalusian, Neapolitan and Oriental blood to produce a heavy, useful horse. This was valued by farmers for its strength and reliability, and as a

LEFT & OPPOSITE: The quality of Holstein breeding stock is ensured through annual inspections, when horses are evaluated and graded.

military horse for its courage, stamina, and ability. It was also favored as a coaching horse. After the Reformation, the monastery land was returned to the landowners who continued the horse-breeding tradition.

By 1686 the Holstein had become so respected that strict guidelines were introduced to protect and improve the breed, which was by now popular throughout Europe. By the 18th century the Holstein's reputation had become so great that vast numbers of horses were exported. Unfortunately, not all of them had been bred to the exacting standards that had once prevailed and general deterioration set in.

By the 19th century, fortunately, the decline had been halted, and measures were now being taken to save and improve the breed. As the demand for warhorses grew less, the Holstein came to be used as a quality carriage horse, and to this end, Yorkshire Coach Horses and Cleveland Bay stallions were mated with Holstein mares. This was a great success, and the breed was given a new lease on life.

Thoroughbred was also added to refine the breed after the Second World War, which also improved the Holstein's jumping ability and general character. Today, it is a supreme sporthorse, excelling at dressage, show jumping and eventing. It has also been bred to good effect with other warmblood breeds, most effectively with the Hanoverian.

The Holstein is quite different from other warmbloods in that it has a large, rangy build resulting in a huge stride. The head is long and straight with large, flaring nostrils. The ears are expressive and the eyes are large and gentle. The long neck is elegant and well-developed, with high withers; the back is long and straight. The shoulders are shapely and sloping, which also contributes to its long stride. The chest is broad, the girth is deep, and the quarters are slightly sloping, muscular, and powerful. The legs are long and muscular.

The Holstein is a fine, well-balanced horse, with an amazing ground-covering, elastic stride. The overall effect is of an elegant horse that carries itself lightly. It is good-natured, obedient, and eager to work. Its large size and scope means that it is much in demand as a top-flight competition horse.

Holsteins are most commonly bay, though all solid colors, together with gray, are permitted. They stand around 16–17 hh.

ICELANDIC

The Icelandic Horse is derived from the Fjord and Døle horses of Norway, and the Celtics, Shetlands, Highlands, and Connemaras of the British Isles, which were brought to Iceland by Scandinavian settlers in the 9th century. Because of the limited space on board their ships, the invaders would have brought only the best specimens, and once settled, would have allowed

LEFT, OPPOSITE & OVERLEAF:
Icelandics are tireless and efficient movers, making them ideal for trail rides and treks.

their horses to mate freely, producing the Icelandic breed as we know it today. This resulted in a hardy animal, able to tolerate semi-wild conditions and to survive harsh Arctic winters. It was used mainly for farming and for riding over icy terrain.

The Icelandic has been bred in closed pedigrees since the Middle Ages, because it must be traceable back to its Icelandic ancestors. Even though it is a pony in stature, it is always referred to as a horse; this is because there is no word for pony in the Icelandic language. It is often mentioned in the Icelandic Sagas, where to a warrior, a good horse was worth more than gold. Great horses were treated with respect and slain warriors would often have been buried alongside their mounts.

Icelandics have lately been exported to other countries, however, where cross-breeding has been allowed to take place.

This is a well-constructed animal. The head is of medium length, having a typical pony character with small pricked ears and soft, expressive eyes. The neck is well-set, and the chest is broad with a deep girth. The body and legs are stocky and strong and the feet are extremely hard.

The Icelandic is ideal for children, being tough, hardy, and happy to live out all-year-round. It has two extra gaits: the *tølt*, which is a running walk with four beats, and is as fast as a canter and very comfortable; and the flying pace, which has two beats and is used for racing but which makes great demands on horse and rider. Speeds of up to 30 mph (48km/h) can be reached using the flying pace, and to witness this is impressive indeed. The Icelandic is late to mature, however, and should not be backed until it is four years old. It can live to a ripe old age, often working up until 30; in fact, an Icelandic in Britain is known to have died aged 42.

Icelandics come in all solid colors as well as skewbald, palomino, dun, and gray. A silver dapple coat is much prized; this is where the body is a rich brown and the mane and tail appear almost silver by contrast. In winter the coat is very thick, with three distinct layers. Icelandics stand between 12 and 13.2 hh, and have been known to reach 14.2 hh.

"I heard a neigh. Oh, such a brisk and melodious neigh as that was! My very heart leaped with delight at the sound."

Nathaniel Hawthorne

KLADRUBER

This old breed was established in 1597 by the Emperor Maximilian II of Austria, where it was bred at the Kladruber Stud which is situated in the former Czechoslovakia. Today the stud still produces Kladruber horses which are a mix of many different breeds. Heavy Alpine mares were originally mated with Barb and Turkish stallions, then later with Andalusian,

LEFT & OVERLEAF: Kladrubers are often used in modern competitive carriage driving and have been highly successful in this discipline.

Neapolitan, and Lipizzaner, resulting in horses that were used exclusively to draw coaches and appear in parades of the Austrian Court in Vienna.

But the Second World War eventually took its toll on the breed with numbers plummeting to dangerously low levels; it was therefore decided to revive and improve the breed by adding Anglo-Norman, Hanoverian, and Oldenburg bloodlines, which were mixed with the remaining stock. Today, the Kladruber is doing well and is used for general riding and for light haulage.

The Kladruber has inherited many of the attributes of the Andalusian, Neapolitan, and Lipizzaner. The head is noble with a broad forehead, straight or slightly Roman nose, medium well-shaped ears, and an alert expression with large, kind and intelligent eyes. The neck is high-set and well-developed; the girth is deep and the chest broad. The body is of medium length and is sturdy with large quarters. The legs are well-muscled with good bone and well-shaped hooves.

The Kladruber has an equable temperament and is a willing and obedient worker. It has an attractive high-stepping action.

They are usually gray in color, though blacks are also bred. Height is 16.2–17 hh.

—◇—

KNABSTRUP

The Knabstrup's ancestry can be traced back, possibly to prehistoric Iberian horses. The Knabstrup is unusual for a European horse in that it has a distinctive spotted coat. This is thought to have been inherited from its prehistoric forebears, many of which can be seen depicted in primitive cave paintings.

LEFT & OVERLEAF: The Knabstrup is beginning to make itself known in the show ring and in many competitive equestrian sports.

Spotted horses were very popular at the courts of European royalty in the 16th and 17th centuries; but the Knabstrup was founded much later, in the early 1800s, when an Iberian mare of the Knabstrup Estate in Denmark was mated with a palomino Frederiksborg stallion. The foal was born with a spotted coat of many colors, which also had an attractive sheen. This horse became the foundation stallion of the Knabstrup breed.

Unfortunately, because subsequent horses were bred primarily for their unusual coats, insufficient care and attention was given to their conformation, leading to gradual deterioration when the breed subsequently lost its popularity and almost disappeared. The horse has been improved in recent years, however, and the addition of Thoroughbred bloodlines has made it popular once more. Today it is used as a general riding horse and also features in showing classes and even circuses, due to its spotted coat.

The head is large, with a straight or Roman nose. The ears are small and well-pricked and the eyes have a kind, gentle expression. The muzzle is square, with large, open nostrils. The neck is high-set, the shoulders are well-developed, and the chest is broad. The back is rather long, with slightly sloping quarters, and the legs are strong with plenty of good bone. The mane and tail are rather sparse.

With its excellent natural paces, the Knabstrup is a good-quality riding horse. It is complaisant and intelligent, easy to train, and is an obedient and willing worker.

Colors and patterns are various, with permutations similar to those present in the Appaloosa. Full leopard spotting is the most highly prized, though one overall color or roan are also possible. Height is 15.2 hh.

LEFT & OPPOSITE: The beautiful and spotted coat of the Knabstrup occurs in many colors and variations. Despite its increasing popularity, it is still relatively rare.

LIPIZZANER

The Lipizzaner, due to its association with the Spanish Riding School of Vienna, is one of the world's most recognizable breeds. Despite its origins in what is now Slovenia, the Lipizzaner has a far more ancient history, dating back to the 8th century and the Moorish occupation of

LEFT & OVERLEAF: The Lipizzaner is a long-lived breed, but slow to mature. They are born dark or black in color but most become lighter through a graying process. By the time they are between 6 and 10 years of age the vast majority are completely white.

Spain. The Moors brought horses of Oriental origin to Spain, such as Arabs and Barbs. These were bred with the heavier Iberian horses, which in turn produced the Andalusian – the most important element in the Lipizzaner's line of heredity.

In 1580 Archduke Charles, son of the Holy Roman Emperor Ferdinand I, who had inherited Austria-Hungary, sought to improve his horses, and decided on the system of haute école, or the practice of advanced classical dressage. He founded a stud at Lipizza for the purpose, which also specialized in breeding carriage horses, and filled it with quality Spanish (Iberian) horses, known to be capable of the discipline. He used these horses as the foundation stock of the Lipizzaner, crossing them with heavier native breeds, together with Barb, Arab, Andalusian, Neapolitan, and Kladruber. Thus, over a period of several hundred years, the classic riding horse was born.

The illustrious Spanish Riding School had been founded in Vienna in 1572. It got its name, not because of its Spanish riding traditions but because of the Spanish origins of its horses. The aim of the school was to teach the art of classical equestrianism to men of noble breeding. The original venue had been a crude wooden structure, which was eventually replaced by the splendid building that was commissioned by Charles VI in 1735 and which is still in use today. The Spanish Riding School is now stocked exclusively with Lipizzaner stallions.

When the Austro-Hungarian Empire collapsed, the stud was moved to Piber in Austria, and during the Second World War was evacuated to Germany for its own protection. Today, Lipizzaners are bred mainly at Piber (which supplies all the stallions for the Spanish Riding School), though some also come from Lipizza and Babolna in Hungary, and from the Czech Republic, Slovenia, and Romania. Nowadays, as well as performing in the Spanish Riding School, Lipizzaners are also used as draft horses, for carriage driving, and are becoming popular as general riding horses.

The Lipizzaner breed was based on six foundation stallions, and their different characteristics can be seen in their descendants to this day. Lipizzaners can therefore vary according to which of the six bloodlines were used, but generally speaking they are of an Iberian type, similar to the Lusitano and Andalusian.

The head is large with either a straight or Roman nose. The ears are finely pointed and alert and the eyes kind and intelligent. The neck is well-set, powerful and well-muscled with a good crest. The chest is wide with a

deep girth. The shoulders can be slightly straight and short. The back is long but strong and muscular, with powerful quarters and a slightly low-set tail. The legs are shortish but powerful, with small, well-shaped, tough hooves.

The noble Lipizzaner possesses all the admirable qualities of its breeding: the agility and balance of its Iberian forebears, as well as the stamina and refinement of the Orientals. It combines stamina with natural balance and agility, is kind, intelligent, willing, and obedient but with plenty of sparkle. Lipizzaners are late to mature, usually around the age of 7, and should not be worked too young. They remain sound for a relatively long time, however, and usually live to a good age.

Lipizzaners are famous for their gray (white) coats. Foals are born dark, but most lighten to become pure white on reaching maturity. Very few remain brown or black. They stand between 15 and 15.3 hh.

Some non-white Lipizzaners have traditionally been kept at the Spanish Riding School as reminders of the white Lipizzaners' bay, black, brown, or roan Spanish forebears.

All modern Lippizaners can be traced back to the foundation bloodstock of the breed. The majority of Lipizzaners reside in Europe, with smaller numbers in the Americas, Africa, and Australia.

LUSITANO

Sharing its heritage with the Andalusian, the Lusitano is also descended from the Iberian riding horse. The Lusitano gets its name (adopted only in the early 20th century) from Lusitania, which was the Roman name for Portugal. The origins of the breed date to around 25,000 BC and to the ancient ancestors of the Sorraia pony, which can be seen in cave paintings throughout the Iberian Peninsula.

LEFT & OVERLEAF: The Portugese Lusitano shares much of its ancestry with the Spanish Andalusian.

Unlike the Andalusian, the Lusitano's breeding has remained truer to its Sorraia ancestry, in that it has only received infusions of Oriental, Garrano, and Spanish blood. To keep the breed true to type, this mix hasn't been changed for centuries and care is taken to use only horses with obvious Iberian characteristics.

The Lusitano was bred mainly for agricultural use around the fertile River Tagus, where it is still used for the purpose. It is also used in bullfighting, as well as in haute école. Thankfully, in Portugal, the bull is not killed, and the entire business takes place with the rider on the horse's back. However, the Lusitano has to be incredibly agile and fast to avoid injury.

These horses are highly prized and receive haute école training to enhance their precision so that they can survive the demanding and dangerous spectacle. The Lusitano stallions are trained to these high standards before they are sent to stud, and all fighting horses are left entire; it is believed that geldings lack the courage and intelligence to work in the bullring.

Today, the horse is also used in all levels of dressage. Infusions of Lusitano are also used to improve other breeds.

The Lusitano has a fine, noble countenance. The head is quite long, with a straight or slightly Roman nose and flared nostrils. The ears are of medium length, well-shaped, and alert. The eyes are keen and intelligent, the neck is set high, with a well-developed muscular crest, and well-defined withers. The sloping shoulders are powerful and the chest is broad with a deep girth. The back is short and strong and the loins broad, with quarters that are not too large. The Lusitano's high-stepping action is attributed to its strong, long hocks, which are capable of great impulsion, and the deep flexion is achieved by a well-developed second thigh (stifle).

This noble and courageous horse is kind, good-natured, and obedient. It is level-headed and not given to sudden panic, which are important attributes in a fighting horse. Lusitanos have competed in several Olympics and World Equestrian Games as part of the Portuguese and Spanish dressage teams.

They may be any solid color as well as gray, and they stand between 15 and 16 hh.

SHETLAND

Lying off the north-eastern coast of Scotland, the Shetlands consist of over 100 offshore islands. The islands are remote and have a harsh climate, particularly in winter, and there is not much shelter for the ponies that inhabit them. Food is scarce, but the ponies have adapted to survive on very little. They live on next to nothing during the winter months, but it is known that they come down from the hills to feed on the seaweed that has been washed up on the beaches.

It is unclear where these ponies originated, but there is evidence from Bronze Age remains that they have been present for a very long time, probably descended from the Celtic Pony. Alternatively, they may have crossed the ice from Scandinavia, or may even have come from Europe.

LEFT, OPPOSITE & OVERLEAF: Today, the famous Shetland is usually used as a children's riding pony or driven for competition or pleasure.

Traditionally, Shetlands were used by islanders as riding, plowing, pack, and harness ponies. In 1870, the Londonderry Stud at Bressay, Scotland, fixed the type and character of the breed and today's best stock can still be traced to the famous Londonderry sires, even though the stud no longer exists.

The Shetland's head is small and neat and can be slightly dished. The ears are small and the eyes open and bold. The neck, shoulders, and withers are well-defined; the chest and quarters must be strong and muscular. The mane and tail is profuse, with straight feathering on the legs. The coat is double-layered – a feature unique to the Shetland Pony.

The Shetland has plenty of character and can be willful on occasions. Because it is relatively strong for its size, unless it has been properly trained and has good manners, it may be too much for a small child. But when kept in a suitable environment, with adult help on hand, Shetlands make superb children's ponies.

Shetlands can be most colors, and black, brown, bay, chestnut, gray, piebald, and skewbald are all common.

Standard Shetlands grow to a maximum height of 42 inches (107cm). Since the 1980s, however, a miniature Shetland has been developed which does not exceed 34 inches (86cm).

THOROUGHBRED

The history of the Thoroughbred dates to the 17th century, when English farmers and landowners became increasingly interested in racing. Until that time, local horses, not having been specifically bred for the purpose, were being raced, and it soon became apparent that a selective breeding program was required to make them more suitable for the task. This became more urgent as gambling became popular with the public at large.

The wealthier landowners realized that while the native horses had stamina, they were lacking in speed, so between 1689 and 1729, in order to improve the stock, they began to import horses from the Middle East. It is generally accepted that the modern Thoroughbred stems from three such stallions: the Byerley Turk, the Darley Arabian, and the Godolphin Arabian, all of which had a long experience of working at stud. Between them, they established the three bloodlines of Herod, Eclipse, and Matchem, which were pivotal to the British Thoroughbred – a name not applied to the breed until 1821.

OPPOSITE: All Thoroughbreds are registered in the General Stud Book that was started in 1791.

Although initially bred with racing in mind, the qualities of the Thoroughbred make it an ideal horse for all other equestrian disciplines, e.g., eventing, show jumping, dressage, etc. Not only has the Thoroughbred been exported far and wide to improve racing stocks, it has also been used to improve hundreds of other breeds around the world.

Descendants of the three foundation sires reached the United States in the 1730s, where

LEFT & OPPOSITE: Thoroughbreds are used mainly for racing, but also compete in other equestrian disciplines. They make excellent eventers and dominate the sport.

they were generally similar to Thoroughbreds elsewhere; recently, however, a distinctive American type has emerged, with longer hindlegs and a longer stride, making its quarters appear higher in comparison.

The Thoroughbred is a beautiful and athletic animal, with long, clean limbs, a fine, silky coat, an elegant profile, and a muscular body. The eyes are always large and intelligent and the ears finely sculpted. Built for toughness, stamina, and speed, the Thoroughbred is regarded as the ultimate racing machine.

Thoroughbreds are courageous, honest, and bold, and one only has to be present at a steeplechase or hurdle race to see that this is so. The Thoroughbred is often described as "hot-headed," and while this may be true of some individuals, which are more sensitive than others, most are a pleasure to own and ride.

Pure-bred and Thoroughbred are not synonymous in this context: the latter, in this case, is the actual name of this breed.

All true colors are acceptable, and height is usually between 15 and 16.2 hh.

—

TRAKEHNER

The Trakehner has had a checkered history dating to 1732, when the first Trakehner stud was founded in East Prussia, part of the former kingdom of Prussia and now in Poland. The stud became the main source of stallions for the whole of Prussia and the area quickly became famous for its beautiful and elegant coach horses.

LEFT & OPPOSITE: Owing to its Throroughbred ancestry, the Trakehner is spirited, athletic, and trainable with plenty of stamina.

The breed came into being when native horses of the region were bred with Thoroughbreds and Arabs, infusions which gave the Trakehner its speed and endurance. Within 50 years, however, the emphasis had shifted from producing coach horses to breeding chargers for the cavalry, which continued until the Second World War, when the Trakehner stud was completely destroyed. Fortunately, toward the end of the war, about 1,000 horses were saved when they were trekked west, accompanied by refugees escaping from the Russian invasion. Although some of the horses died on the way, due to the harsh conditions, sufficient survived to continue the breed. Today, the breeding of the Trakehner is again flourishing in its place of origin as well as in other countries.

In terms of appearance, the Trakehner resembles the middleweight Thoroughbred. The head is fine, with an intelligent and interested expression. The profile is straight and similar to that of the Thoroughbred. The neck and shoulders are shapely, the back short and strong, and the quarters powerful. The legs are strong and straight, producing a powerful, straight action.

The Trakehner has an excellent temperament, being amiable, obedient, and courageous. Although it resembles the Thoroughbred, it is without the "hot" temperament associated with that breed. For this reason, breeders looking for an infusion of Thoroughbred without this trait often select Trakehner stallions instead. The Trakehner is the most elegant of the warmbloods and is the nearest in character to the Thoroughbred. Nowadays, because of its athleticism and paces, it is predominantly used for competition, particularly dressage and eventing.

All solid colors are acceptable and height is usually around 16–16.2 hh.

—✺—

"He's the color of the nutmeg. And of the heat of the ginger ... he is pure air and fire; and the dull elements of earth and water never appear in him, but only in patient stillness while his rider mounts him; he is indeed a horse, and all other jades you may call beasts."

William Shakespeare

THE WELSH BREEDS

Native ponies were present in Wales as much as 10,000 years ago. At that time, the indigenous breed inhabiting the hills was the Celtic Pony, and it is thought that all Welsh ponies known today derive from this ancient breed.

It is recorded that native stock was being bred in Wales in around 50 BC, when Julius Caesar founded a stud in Merionethshire and was responsible for

LEFT: A Welsh Mountain Pony (Section A).

OVERLEAF: A Welsh Pony of Cob type (Section C).

introducing Arab blood into the breed. The first mention of Welsh ponies and cobs appears in the laws of Hywel Dda, written in AD 930.

Throughout the centuries, variations on the original wild ponies were developed. Early on in the 20th century, the Welsh Pony and Cob Society identified the four clear types. These are the original, once wild, Welsh Mountain Pony not exceeding 12 hh (Section A); the Welsh Pony not exceeding 13 hh (Section B); the Welsh Pony of Cob Type up to 13.2 hh (Section C); the Welsh Cob of 13.2–15.2 hh (Section D).

The Welsh Mountain Pony (Section A) is the oldest of all the Welsh breeds. As the name suggests it is tough, resilient, sound in limb as well as constitution. Known for its intelligence, agility, endurance, and hardiness, the Welsh Mountain Pony is capable of surviving the harshest of winters. These ponies are now found all over the world and are highly regarded as quality children's riding ponies; they also perform well in harness.

The head is refined, with a slim tapering muzzle and small, pricked ears. The eyes are large and bold. These qualities, as well as a dished face, give the Welsh Mountain a distinct resemblance to the Arab, a breed that has been introduced. The neck, well-defined withers, and quarters are in proportion to the rest of the pony's body, while the tail is set quite high. The limbs are set square, with well-made joints, and the feet are small, rounded, and hard.

The Welsh Mountain has great personality and charm, having inherited intelligence and quick-wittedness – traits which the original wild ponies seemed to have possessed in abundance. When in action, the gaits should be smooth and the hocks well-flexed. They are usually gray, but all true colors are acceptable.

The Welsh Pony (Section B) has all the best attributes of the Welsh Mountain Pony, though breeders have accentuated its talents as a riding pony. Moreover, because the Welsh Pony has been used for generations on farms for herding sheep, it has similar toughness and agility.

These qualities, when combined with good looks, jumping ability, and superb conformation for riding, makes them perfect as children's mounts.

The Welsh Pony shares many similarities with the Welsh Mountain Pony. The head is refined, with small pricked ears, and the face may be slightly dished. The eyes are large and intelligent. The neck, back, and quarters are muscular and in proportion, and the tail is set high. The limbs are straight and strong and the hooves strong and rounded.

The Welsh Pony is willing, active, and enthusiastic and will always give of its best. Like the Welsh Mountain they are predominantly gray, but all true colors are acceptable.

The Welsh Pony of Cob Type (Section C) was originally used for farm work – also for carting slate from the mines. It is of a similar height to the Welsh Pony, but sturdier and capable of carrying heavier loads. It was developed more as a harness pony than for ridden work and has a naturally pronounced action, probably inherited from the Hackney, which was introduced into the breed.

General appearance is of a small cob. The eyes are spaced widely apart and the expression is intelligent. Like the others, the ears are small and pricked. The body and legs are sturdier and more cob-like than those of the Welsh Pony, and the feet are slightly larger. Mane and tail are full.

The Welsh Pony of Cob Type is similar in temperament to the other Welsh breeds, being lively and enthusiastic. It performs well in harness and is also a natural jumper.

All true colors are acceptable, but for the show ring, ponies are preferred with plenty of white on the lower legs.

Of all the Welsh breeds, the Welsh Cob (Section D) is the most famous. Known for its handsome appearance and extravagant paces, not

OPPOSITE: A Welsh Pony of Cob type (Section C).

OVERLEAF: A Welsh Cob (Section D) stallion.

only is it the ultimate working cob, it is also guaranteed to command attention in the show ring.

The breed dates from the 11th century, when it was known as the Powys Cob or Powys Rouncy. Welsh Cobs not only possess Welsh Mountain Pony blood, they were also influenced by imports from all over the Roman Empire. Breeds from Spain, such as the Andalusian, and the Barb and Arab from North Africa, were all crossed with the early Welsh Cob variety. Later in the 18th and 19th centuries other breeds, such as Hackney and Yorkshire Coach Horse, were also introduced.

Welsh Cobs were traditionally used by the military as well as by farmers, but they were so versatile that they could be used by virtually anyone needing transport or light haulage.

The Welsh Cob is compact, well-muscled, well-balanced, and strong. It has a fine head with large, intelligent eyes, and the usual small, pricked ears. The neck is arched and muscular, the back is short-coupled for strength, and the quarters are powerful and rounded. The legs are sturdy and straight and the hard and rounded feet are in proportion with the animal's body.

The Welsh Cob is proud, courageous, and extravagant in action. It is suitable for all disciplines and for all riders.

All true colors are acceptable.

HORSES OF
EASTERN EUROPE

DON

The Don originated in the harsh Russian steppes, where it once roamed in herds, surviving the freezing winters and torrid summers with nothing but sparse vegetation for food.

The original steppes breed, known as the Old Don, was bred with various Orientals, such as the Arab, Karabakh and

LEFT & OVERLEAF: Originally used as a cavalry horse for the Cossacks, the Don is now widely used as a saddle horse and is also driven. Known for its endurance and stamina, it can cover long distances with ease.

Turkmene, and Orlov and Thoroughbred were added to improve its conformation and provide it with incredible stamina.

The horse was the preferred mount of the Don Cossacks; it was also used by the Russian army, and its extreme toughness made it particularly popular with wolf-hunters. Today, the Don's hardy constitution makes it an excellent endurance horse. It is also used to improve other breeds.

The overall picture of the Don is one of strength and robustness. The head is fairly small and neat, the slightly dished or straight nose clearly indicating its Arab heritage. Ears are small and shapely and the eyes are large and intelligent. The neck is set high and should be arched; however, many have ewe necks. The back is fairly long, straight, and wide, with sloping quarters and a straight shoulder. The legs are clean but in some cases can be sickle-hocked. Moreover, the placement of the pelvis tends to restrict movement and causes a stilted action – a fault that has now been largely bred out. The hooves are well-shaped and hard.

Tough and sturdy, with an independent spirit, these qualities have found their way into other breeds. The most striking feature of the Don's coat is its iridescent sheen. It is most commonly chestnut, but can also be bay, brown, black, and gray. It stands approximately 15.2 hh.

KABARDIN

Originating in the Caucasus, the Kabardin is descended from the Tarpan – the wild horse of Eastern Europe and Asia, which sadly became extinct in captivity in 1887. The Kabardin remained unchanged in type until the Russian Revolution when, like many other Russian horses, steps were taken to improve the breed. The original Kabardin was bred with Karabakh, Turkmene, Persian, and Arab to create a

The Kabardin has a strong constitution and a hardiness that allows it to thrive in extreme climates.

much bigger, stronger horse, suitable for riding and general farm work, and also for use as a packhorse. The Kabardin is also an excellent mountain horse – possibly the best there is – being sure-footed, agile, and intelligent, with the innate ability to search out the safest routes. Its great stamina enables it to work all day without becoming stressed.

The breed remains popular in its place of origin to this day. This is now the Republic of Kabardino-Balkaria, where it is still used for light draft work and for riding. Elsewhere, it is used in competition and to improve other breeds.

The Kabardin has a longish head, often with a slightly Roman nose. The longish ears point inwards and are set close together. The eyes are wise and intelligent and the nostrils flared. The neck is long and well-developed, and the back is straight and strong; the legs are long and fine, but at the same time also very strong. The overall impression is of a horse with strong Oriental influences.

Kabardins are kind, obedient, intelligent, and trustworthy. They are a hardy breed, and with extra feeding can live out all year. They have strong constitutions and mostly live to a ripe old age.

Colors may be bay, black, brown, and very occasionally gray. Height is somewhere between 14.2 and 15.1 hh.

KONIK

The Konik, or "little horse," with its primitive markings, resembles the wild Tarpan of eastern Europe and western Asia which is now extinct. The Konik itself is not a specific breed and there is no particular standard, but there are around five types, some with native blood and others with added Arab bloodlines.

The Konik, being related to the Tarpan, which was a small horse of Oriental origin, has a small, neat head, dorsal stripe, and zebra markings. Sadly, the last remaining Tarpan died in captivity in 1887, having been hunted to extinction some ten years earlier.

In the last century, efforts were made to revive the ancient breed by preserving the Konik's Tarpan genes. These reconstituted Tarpans, as they are now known, live wild in a nature reserve where they are beginning to manifest many Tarpan characteristics. Today Koniks are mainly used for farm work and occasionally as children's ponies.

The Konik has a strong head with great character that shows its Oriental origins. The neck is of medium length and quite thick but with a good carriage. The body is stout and sturdy with well-developed, medium-length legs, which are slightly feathered. The hooves are tough.

The Konik is hardy and will live out all year round with little extra feeding and care. Some can be willful and difficult – a throwback to their wild Tarpan origins. Usually light-brown or dun and sometimes bay, the mane and tail are full and the dorsal stripe and zebra markings are sometimes visible. Height is 12.2–13.3 hh.

ORLOV TROTTER

The Orlov, (or Orloff) Trotter, with its hereditary fast trot, is one of the foremost breeds of its type in the world. It was founded in the 18th century by Count Alexey Orlov, whose ambition it was to produce a superb trotting horse. He founded a stud at Ostrov, near Moscow, for the purpose, bringing in a large number of Arab horses. One of these was the stallion Smetanka, a silver-gray horse, large and rather

The famous Orlov Trotter has a hereditary fast trot and is renowned for its outstanding speed and stamina. Unfortunately it is now rare.

long-backed for the breed, with
an extravagant trot. After a
season, Orlov was left with a few
progeny, bred from Dutch
Harddraver, Mecklenburg,
Danish, Thoroughbred, and
Arabian mares.

Orlov decided to look for a
better stud farm, with more
grazing, which he found in
Khrenovoye in the Voronezh
region to the south of Moscow.
He considered it perfect for his
purpose, in that there were vast
areas of grassland, clear springs,
and a dry climate.

The Khrenovoye Stud was
thus founded in 1778, and the
following year produced a colt
called Polkan I, which in turn was

mated with a Danish mare carrying Spanish blood. The result was a foal called Bars I, which eventually showed exceptional stamina and trotting abilities and became the foundation stallion of the Orlov breed.

The Orlov is a muscular horse, famous for its exceptional and impressive action. Its stamina and quality ensured that it reigned supreme on the race track until the end of the 19th century, when Standardbreds and later French Trotters were introduced to the scene. Unfortunately, the Orlov is now in crisis, which is largely due to the introduction of these faster breeds.

The Orlov has a small, elegant head, with a noble profile and ears highly reminiscent of those of the Arab horse. The hindquarters are powerful and, like many trotters, the shoulders are straight. It is energetic, sure-footed and bold. Owing to its swift, balanced trot, it is suitable for riding and driving as well as trotting.

Orlovs are usually gray, black, or bay and range from 15.2–17 hh in height.

—m—

SHAGYA ARABIAN

The beautiful Shagya Arabian comes from Hungary's second most famous breeding establishment, the Babolna Stud, founded in the late 1700s; the other is the Mezöhegyes Stud.

In 1816 the military stipulated that all brood mares should be bred with Oriental stallions to provide cavalry and harness horses; stallions with

LEFT, OPPOSITE & OVERLEAF:
Today the Shagya Arabian is now a popular choice for equestrian sports such as dressage, eventing, and endurance riding.

mixed Oriental blood as well as Iberian crosses were also used. The results, although fairly lightweight, were horses that were tough and had a good deal of stamina.

Following this success, it was decided that the Bobolna Stud should concentrate on breeding horses with predominantly Arab blood, which was the beginning of the excellent Shagya Arabian.

Today's breed is descended from one Arab stallion, called Shagya, which was brought from Syria in 1836. He was fairly large for an Arab, standing at 15.2$^{1/2}$ hh, and was from the Siglavi or Seglawy strain. The stallion was typically Arab in conformation, with a fine dished nose, a proud high-crested neck, a short body, and a high-set tail.

It was mated with the military-style mares to produce the first Shagya Arabians and subsequent breeding by selection has produced a beautiful, refined riding horse of the highest possible quality. Today Shagya Arabians make excellent riding and competition horses and are also used for driving. They remain popular in their native land, but are relatively rare elsewhere.

The Shagya is very like the Arab in conformation, but a little heavier. The head is wedge-shaped, with a wide forehead and a straight or dished nose. The ears are neatly pointed and alert, and the eyes are kind. The muzzle is small and delicate, with large flaring nostrils. The neck is beautifully arched, well-muscled, and set high. The shoulders are sloping, with a broad chest and deep girth; the body is fairly short, with well-defined quarters and long, elegant legs; well-muscled at the top, the legs have more bone than those of the traditional Arab.

The Shagya has the constitution of the Arab but is bigger and stronger. It is kind, noble, and spirited, and has great stamina, speed, and agility.

All solid colors are acceptable, although many have inherited the Shagya stallion's gray color. Rarest of all is black. They stand somewhere between 14.2 and 15.2 hh.

—◊◊—

TERSKY

Originating in the Northern Caucasus, the Tersky or Tersk is a true performance horse, specializing in endurance, racing, jumping, and dressage. Not only has it excellent sporting and athletic capabilities, it is also one of the most beautiful of the Russian breeds.

The breed is now concentrated at the Stavropol Stud. Breeding and rearing previously took place on the

Although the Tersky looks refined and fine-coated, its copes well in a harsh climate. It is loyal, intelligent, kind, and courageous.

steppes, with the result that weaker stock succumbed to wolves or died of disease. Learning to survive, therefore, made the breed tough.

The modern breed is a product of the early 20th century; it was based on the Strelets Arab, produced by crossing Anglo-Arabs with Orlovs, and was developed by crossing Arabs with old-type Terskys to which Thoroughbred blood had been also introduced.

There are three variations on the Tersky: the first is lightweight, fine and Arab-like in appearance, and is known as the Eastern type. The second is middleweight, sturdier, and longer in the back, with a frame that is thicker-set, while the third is the heavier type that has received infusions of Trakehner.

The Tersky is a horse of medium height and great beauty, which reflects its Arabian heritage. The head is finely formed with a dished profile; the eyes are large and intelligent and the nostrils flared.

The Tersky has an equable temperament that combines kindness and intelligence with courage and stamina.

They are predominantly gray, usually with a metallic sheen to the coat, while black, chestnut, and bay are also possible. They stand between 15 and 16 hh.

HORSES OF ASIA

AKHAL-TEKE

The Akhal-Teke of
Turkmenistan, a republic in
central Asia lying between the
Caspian Sea and Afghanistan, is
believed to be a descendant of the
Turkoman or Turkmene, an
ancient race of horses thought to
have existed thousands of years
ago, but now unfortunately
extinct. It takes its name from the
Teke tribe, which still inhabits
the Akhal Oasis in the Karakum
Desert, close to the border with

LEFT & OVERLEAF: The Akhal-Teke
is famous for the distinctive metallic
sheen to its coat in some individuals.

Iran. Here the horses are traditionally kept in herds under the watchful eyes of mounted herdsmen. This aristocrat of the desert is long, slim elegance personified, but it also has a hardy constitution and can go for long periods without water. In their protected environment, however, the horses are well-tended by the herdsman, who use heavy rugs to cover their backs during extremes of heat and cold. They were once hand-fed a high-protein diet, which surprisingly included eggs and mutton fat.

Historically, this "heavenly" horse was prized by such warlords as Alexander the Great, Darius the Mede, and Genghis Khan, while Marco Polo praised the Turkoman horse in his *Travels*. Nowadays, because of their great agility and athleticism, Akhal-Tekes are most often used for racing and in endurance events.

The Akhal-Teke appears to break almost every rule of good conformation. Its head is carried high on a long, thin neck set at an angle of 45 degrees to the body, giving it a proud, slightly haughty appearance. It has a fine, elegant head with wide cheeks, and a straight or slightly dished nose; the large eyes are bold and expressive. The nostrils are dry and flared and the ears shapely and alert. Although the shoulders are broad and sloping, the chest is quite narrow. The body is fairly short, rounded, and shallow, and the long loins have little definition. The girth is quite narrow, and the very long legs appear disproportionately long in relation to the body, and taper to small hooves.

It has an unusually smooth-flowing and powerful action. The shape of the pasterns are unique to the breed, possibly developed from negotiating desert terrain.

The Akhal-Teke is not known for its sunny nature, in fact, quite the reverse. It is willful and rebellious and benefits from one firm handler which it can learn to trust. It is an intelligent animal which requires careful and sympathetic training; it does not respond well to punishment and may very well retaliate. Due to its genetic inheritance it is unlikely to flourish cooped up in a stable and must be allowed a predominantly outdoor life, with plenty of space to wander.

Colors may be chestnut, bay, gray, palomino, black, and dun. All the colors, apart from raven black, are strikingly iridescent. Height is approximately 15.2 hh, though, with its pronounced withers and high head-carriage, the horse appears taller.

—〜〜—

"The horse is God's gift to mankind."

Arabian Proverb

ARABIAN

The Arabian (Arab) is one of the oldest and most distinctive of the hotblooded breeds, and its bloodlines are present in many modern horses found throughout Europe and the United States. The name is not strictly accurate, as the original "Arab" may well have been a small Oriental-type wild horse, living in Eastern Europe, the Near East and the Middle East. The Arab was further developed as Islam

LEFT, OPPOSITE & OVERLEAF: The Arabian is one of the most instantly recognizable of all horse breeds.

226

assimilated the breed, and Muslim invaders used it as a cavalry horse. Today's modern Arabians can trace their descent from five foundation mares, known as Al-Khamesh (The Five), said to have been selected for their obedience.

The Arab was also of great importance to the Bedouin, the nomadic tribe of the desert, which can trace its association with the breed to 3000 BC, to the mare Baz and the stallion Hoshaba.

Arab horses were so-named when they were imported from the Arabian Peninsula to Britain in the 19th century. The Arab is also the foundation of the Thoroughbred. Arab blood is therefore highly effective when mixed with other breeds, and usually brings great improvements to any offspring that result.

Arabs are extremely beautiful, with a delicacy that belies their strength and stamina. They shine in riding events, such as dressage, riding horse, and in-hand showing. They also excel in disciplines that rely on strength, such as endurance riding and racing. Arabs have the reputation of being unable to jump, which is quite untrue; they are keen jumpers, but lack the ability to compete at high level.

The head is short and refined, with a dish-shaped profile and a tapered muzzle with large nostrils. The eyes are large, wide-apart, and low-set, and the ears are small, shapely, and set well apart. The jaw is rounded and forms a curved arch where head and neck meet, known as the *mitbah*.

The back is slightly concave, with sloping shoulders, and well-defined withers. The croup is level and the girth deep. The tail is set high. The legs are strong, hard, and clean, with flat knees, short cannons, and well-defined tendons; the hooves are hard and tough. The Arab also has a distinctive skeletal feature, in that it has fewer vertebrae, i.e., 5 lumbar, 17 rib, and 16 tail, compared with 6-18-18 in other breeds, giving it a short-coupled appearance.

The horse's action is as if it were floating on air. Due to their desert origins, Arabs have fine coats and skin which is designed to release heat. Consequently, they require special care in winter, though they are tougher than Thoroughbreds.

Arabs are famous for their intelligence and responsiveness. They are also affectionate and respectful of other animals, also of human beings, being especially good with children. The reverse side of their character is that they are fiery and courageous; they can also be stubborn if asked to do something against their will.

All solid colors are possible, but chestnut and gray are the most common. Arabs usually stand somewhere between 14 and 15.2 hh.

HEAVY HORSES

BRABANT

The Brabant, or Belgian Heavy Draft Horse, comes from the Brabant region of modern Belgium. It is of ancient origin, only slightly more recent than the Ardennais, to which it owes part of its lineage: the other part of its inheritance is thought to have stemmed from the Flanders Horse of the 11th to 16th centuries, which in turn is believed to have been descended from the ancient horses of the Quaternary period. For centuries, Belgian breeders produced their stock by selective breeding, which also included inbreeding.

LEFT & OVERLEAF: The Brabant is still used as a working animal, but it is also popular as a show horse. It can be ridden too.

234

The Brabant's very existence is a direct result of the geology of the area: the rich heavy soil required a horse with great pulling power and big strong joints to enable it to lift its huge feet out of the thick clods of mud. As a result, three distinct bloodlines emerged 100 years ago, which intermingled to create the modern Brabant. These are the Gros de la Dendre, which is muscular and strong with huge legs; the Gris de Nivelles, with good conformation and a certain elegance; and the Colosse de la Mehaigne, which is large and has a lively temperament.

Over the centuries, the Brabant has had an enormous influence on today's modern breeds, much in the same way as the Arab bloodline has been added to improve existing stock. In the Middle Ages the horse was imported all over Europe and its bloodlines are also present in Germany's warmbloods. The Russians introduced native breeds to it to produce working horses and its influence is also present in the Shire, Irish Draft, and Clydesdale, to name but a few. Today, Brabants are still part of the foundation stock for the breeding of warmbloods. They now appear throughout the world, where they are still used in agricultural work, logging, and as dray horses. They also feature in the show ring.

The head is fairly square, with a straight profile, small pricked ears, and deep-set eyes with a kindly expression. The neck is short and very strong and set high with a large crest. The shoulders are sloping and the chest is wide and deep. The body is short, with a well-muscled back, and strong quarters. The legs are fairly long and muscular and the hooves are large, rounded, and tough; not much feathering is present.

The Brabant is so extremely docile as to be described as almost sluggish. But it is willing and obedient, and its pulling power is equal only to that of the Shire, for which it is highly prized. It is a hard worker with plenty of stamina and a strong constitution, and requires relatively little food for its size. Brabants are usually light chestnut with a flaxen mane; also acceptable is red roan, bay, dun, and gray. It is a large animal and stands somewhere between 16.1 and 17 hh.

—⁓—

CLYDESDALE

The Clydesdale is a breed of draft horse originating in Clydesdale in Scotland. The establishment of the breed began in the late 17th century when Lanarkshire farmers and various dukes of Hamilton supposedly imported Flemish stallions, ancestors of the Brabant, to Scotland. The

farmers were skillful breeders and mated them with native heavy draft mares already in existence; over the next 100 years or so, English Shire, Friesian, and Cleveland Bay blood was also added. The result was known as the Clydesdale and it was highly prized as a draft horse. The Clydesdale Horse Society was established in 1877, almost a century and a half after the breed first began to evolve.

LEFT, OPPOSITE & OVERLEAF: The outstanding characteristics of this famous horse are a combination of weight, size, and activity.

The breed soon became popular as a general farm horse and also for hauling loads over long and short distances; Clydesdales could be found in most major cities of Scotland, the North of England, and Northern Ireland, as well as in agricultural areas. In fact, the horse became popular the world over, when considerable numbers were imported to North America, Canada, and Australia.

Clydesdales are very different from the usual heavy draft horses, which tend to be plain-looking and squat; in fact, it looks positively refined, having a short-coupled body, long legs, and a high head-carriage. As with all heavy horses, the Clydesdale breed began to decline with the development of motorized transport and reached an even lower ebb in the 1960s and '70s. A few families kept the breed going, however, and today numbers are rising, although the Clydesdale continues to be classified as "at risk" by the Rare Breeds Society. Today they are highly valued in the show ring as well as in harness; as dray horses, they often take part in displays, and are even used to pull wedding carriages.

The head is proudly held, and the medium, well-shaped ears are pricked and alert; the eyes are kind and intelligent. It has a slightly Roman nose and the nostrils are large. The neck is long and well-set, with a high crest leading to high withers. The back is slightly concave and short and the quarters are well-developed and powerful. The legs are straight and long with plenty of feathering. The feet are large and require careful shoeing if contracted heels are not to develop.

These charming horses are energetic with an alert, cheerful air. They are even-tempered and enjoy company. They are extremely strong with a lively action and a slight tendency to dish.

Clydesdales can be bay, brown, and black and usually have white patches all the way up the legs and under the belly, which can turn roan in places. They are around 16.2 hh, but some males may reach 17 hh or more.

PERCHERON

The Percheron is a breed of draft horse that comes from La Perche in Normandy in northern France. The breed is an ancient one, dating back to 732, when Arab horses, abandoned by the Saracens after their defeat at the Battle of Poitiers, were allowed to breed with the local heavy mares of the region. The Percheron type was the result.

LEFT: The Percheron has had a large part to play in France's long history.

At this time, the horse was much lighter than its modern counterpart and was used for riding as well as for light draft work. The type remained popular until the Middle Ages and the Crusades, when Arab and Barb horses from the Holy Land were mated with Percherons. It was also around this time that the Comte de Perche brought back Spanish horses from his forays in Spain; these were also mated with the Percheron, with further infusions of Andalusian added at a later date.

By the 18th century, the original breed had become almost completely eradicated by additions of Thoroughbred and more Arab; in 1820 two gray Arab stallions were mated with Percheron mares, thus creating the predominantly gray color of the modern-day breed.

By now all the heaviness of the ancient breed had disappeared; consequently, heavy mares from other regions were bred with Percheron stallions to make them more suitable for agriculture and to formulate the breed as it is known today. The lighter Percheron still exists and is used as a heavy riding horse, while the heavy version is still used for farm and forestry work and, in some countries, for pulling drays. It is also popular in the show ring.

Over the years the Percheron has been heavily exported to other countries, such as the U.K., Canada, Australia and other parts of Europe, which has helped in its recognization as one of the world's leading heavy breeds.

The Percheron's head is proud and elegant, for a heavy breed, with a straight nose, broad forehead, expressive eyes, and short, shapely ears. The neck is short to medium, well-developed, and with great strength. The shoulders are nicely sloping and well-shaped, with a broad chest and a deep girth. The Percheron is fairly short in the back, which adds to its strength, with slightly sloping but broad quarters. The legs are short and sturdy, with well-shaped tough hooves with very little feather.

The Percheron possesses a good deal of elegance due to the large amounts of Arab blood that have been added over the centuries. It has an excellent temperament, is calm, obedient, and easy to handle, and has a keen intelligence. It has a smooth but lively action which makes it comfortable to ride.

Mainly gray, Percherons can occasionally be black or dark chestnut. There are two types: the small Percheron, which stands between 14.1 and 16.1 hh, and the large, which is somewhere between 16.1 and 17.3 hh.

—m—

OPPOSITE: The larger version of the breed is still used for heavy work.

SHIRE

The English Shire is one of the largest and most majestic breeds in the world. Descended from medieval warhorses, whose immense strength enabled them to carry knights into battle wearing full armor, it was probably based on the Friesian horse, with later infusions of Brabant. It was brought to England by the Dutch to drain the fens of East Anglia, but it was

LEFT & OPPOSITE: Though rare, Shires are occasionally used on the farm. More often, they are used in plowing competitions, in pairs by breweries, or in the show ring.

246

not until the late 19th century that the best heavy horses in England were selected to develop the breed as it is known today.

The Shire's strength also made it suitable for agriculture and heavy haulage work, so initially the breed was established in Lincolnshire and Cambridgeshire, where strong horses were required to cope with heavy fenland soil; but the Shire soon became widespread in Staffordshire, Leicestershire and Derbyshire, until it eventually spread over England as a whole.

Up until the 1930s, the Shire was widely seen across the country, but numbers dropped dramatically when mechanization of farming began to appear, putting the breed in danger of disappearing altogether. Fortunately, the problem was detected by a few dedicated breeders, who helped to promote the breed and restore it to its former glory.

The Shire Horse Society has worked tirelessly to raise funds and encourage the spread of the breed to other countries. Today, there are active Shire Horse societies across Europe, the United States, Canada, and Australia. Although a few Shires are still used on farms today, they are kept mainly for the sheer pleasure of working them in their traditional roles. They are also used in plowing competitions, again, for pleasure, and for the same reason are used in pairs by breweries to deliver beer locally; the spectacle obviously makes for excellent publicity.

The Shire's most significant feature is its sheer size and massive muscular conformation. It is the largest and strongest horse in the world and weighs a ton or more when mature. Built ultimately for strength, the chest is wide, the back short-coupled, the loins and quarters massive. The legs, joints, and feet are sufficiently large to balance and support the Shire's weight; the lower legs are covered with long, straight, silky feathers. In the show ring, white feathers are generally preferred as they help to accentuate the horse's action. Even though the Shire is such a large horse, it is not an ungainly heavyweight; in fact it is very much in proportion and quite awesome to behold. The head is always noble, the nose slightly Roman, and the eyes are large and wise.

The Shire is well-known for its patient, gentle, and placid nature; it is a true "gentle giant." In fact, it is quite amazing that such a strong animal weighing so much can be so easily handled, and it is not uncommon to see them ridden or handled by children or small women. Its kindness is legendary.

Black, brown, and gray are the recognized colors of the breed. White feathers on the legs are preferred for the show ring, and white face markings are common. They stand somewhere between 16.2 and 18 hh.

SUFFOLK PUNCH

The Suffolk Horse, usually known as the Suffolk Punch, originated in East Anglia in England. It takes its name from the county of Suffolk, while "punch" is an old word meaning "short and thickset." It is thought to date back to 1506 and is the oldest heavy breed in Britain.

LEFT & OVERLEAF: While the great warhorses of medieval times were still locked in mortal combat on the battlefield, East Anglian farmers were quietly developing their very own breed of heavy horse — the Suffolk Punch.

The breed was first developed by crossing the native heavy mares of the region with imported French Norman stallions. Modern-day Suffolks, however, can be traced back on the male side to a single, nameless stallion, foaled in 1768 and belonging to Thomas Crisp of Orford, near Woodbridge, Suffolk. Even though the breed is relatively pure, infusions of Norfolk Trotter, Thoroughbred, and Cob were added during the centuries that followed.

Immensely strong, it is also quite agile, due to its relatively small size. These qualities, combined with a lack of feather on the legs, like the Percheron, made it ideal for working the heavy clay soils of East Anglia. Moreover, its economical food consumption, in proportion to its size, enabled it to work for long days on the farm without stopping.

As with many of the heavy breeds, numbers fell dangerously low when farm tractors became widespread. Today, Suffolks are rare, even though there has been a concerted effort to increase numbers in recent years. Today, Suffolks are shown, used in plowing competitions, or are kept by breweries for their novelty value.

The Suffolk Punch is always chestnut in color (the traditional spelling in this instance is chesnut, without the "t"). The breed is well-known for its great strength, and its extremely powerful, muscular body, with relatively short legs,

provides a low center of gravity; this enables the horse to pull plows or vehicles that much more easily. Suffolks mature early and can do light work when they are 2 years old. They continue working well into their 20s.

The Suffolk is docile and hardworking. It is capable of almost any kind of work and is easy to maintain. Height is between 16.1 and 17.1 hh.

INDEX